The Hard Truth

Problems and Issues in Urban School Reform

Sean B. Yisrael

ROWMAN & LITTLEFIELD EDUCATION
A division of
ROWMAN & LITTLEFIELD PUBLISHERS, INC.
Lanham • New York • Toronto • Plymouth, UK

Published by Rowman & Littlefield Education
A division of Rowman & Littlefield Publishers, Inc.
A wholly owned subsidiary of The Rowman & Littlefield Publishing Group, Inc.
4501 Forbes Boulevard, Suite 200, Lanham, Maryland 20706
www.rowman.com

10 Thornbury Road, Plymouth PL6 7PP, United Kingdom

Copyright © 2012 by Sean B. Yisrael

All rights reserved. No part of this book may be reproduced in any form or by any electronic or mechanical means, including information storage and retrieval systems, without written permission from the publisher, except by a reviewer who may quote passages in a review.

British Library Cataloguing in Publication Information Available

Library of Congress Cataloging-in-Publication Data

Yisrael, Sean B.
The hard truth : problems and issues in urban school reform / Sean Yisrael.
pages cm
Includes bibliographical references.
ISBN 978-1-4758-0003-6 (cloth : alk. paper) — ISBN 978-1-4758-0004-3 (pbk. : alk. paper) — ISBN 978-1-4758-0005-0 (ebook) (print)
1. Urban schools—United States. 2. School improvement programs—United States. I. Title.
LC5131.Y58 2012
371.009173'2—dc23
2012010446

™ The paper used in this publication meets the minimum requirements of American National Standard for Information Sciences Permanence of Paper for Printed Library Materials, ANSI/NISO Z39.48-1992.

Printed in the United States of America

Contents

Preface		v
Acknowledgments		ix
Introduction		xi
1	The Leadership Void in Today's Urban Schools	1
2	Conflict and Friction	7
3	Individual Entrapments	13
4	School Culture	17
5	Irate Parents	21
6	Troublemakers on the Staff	29
7	Stagnation and Inefficiency	39
8	Disruptive Students	45
9	Academic Instruction	55
10	Standardized Testing	61
11	Central Office Staff	73
12	The School's Budget	75
13	Social Media	79
14	Practice Self-Reflection	81
Conclusion		85
Bibliography		89
About the Author		91

Preface

This book is a prequel to another book I've written, called *The 12 Laws of Urban School Leadership*. The inspiration for both books came from an unpublished qualitative case study that I completed in 2004 while finishing my master's degree in school administration and leadership.

The study was conducted to determine how school principals perceive their roles as change agents within an urban school model. The participants were all administrators who were either principals working within urban/inner-city schools at the time of the study or former urban school principals who occupied central office administrative positions.

The time I spent with the participants affected me profoundly. Initially, I wanted to do the study because I thought it would be a great leadership topic to explore. Since the start of my educational career, I've always had a sincere interest in public education—urban schools in particular. The basis for my interest in urban schools stems from my personal background.

I attended urban schools from kindergarten through 12th grade. After college, I was employed by an urban school district as a teacher and then later as a school administrator. While conducting the qualitative case study, I had no idea that the information I collected would remain with me and transform the way I viewed the principalship and school reform.

The most impactful information I learned came from the participants' incredible stories. I learned from the stories not only because of their vivid and candid nature but also because they spoke about issues directly effecting urban (and public) education that are not commonly addressed secularly.

The participants' stories also exposed the politics associated with urban school districts. I learned that in most cases, it is the politics of education that impedes the change process more than any other factors. The participants also spoke to matters that happen behind the senses—things that directly affect the school principal's role in fostering effective changes and building a successful school with a culture conducive for learning.

During the study, I acquired two forms of education regarding school administrative leadership: one from graduate school classes that were heavily grounded in theory and ethics and another that was more practical and based in the current realities of the urban school principalship. The theory and ethics side of my graduate school education was beneficial and necessary for my development as a school leader, but in many ways, it only scratched the surface of many topics that the participants of the study described in candid detail.

The information that I learned from the participants in the study gave me a more visceral connection to the urban school principalship; it informed me of the various issues associated with the position; and it gave me a deeper understanding of the challenges that urban school principals face while trying to serve as a catalyst for effective change.

Schools located in urban/inner-city areas are some of the lowest-performing schools in the United States. Most principals who lead them are faced with the twofold problem of having to contend with detrimental community/environmental issues (gangs, excessive and senseless violence, teenage pregnancy, drugs, unemployment, dysfunctional families, single parent homes, etc.) as well as a host of student-teacher issues within the school (low staff morale, union and contract issues, severe student behavioral problems, school violence, drug use and distribution, insufficient budgets, teacher retention issues and layoffs, little to no parental support or involvement, disorganization, low student performance, high dropout rates, inefficiency, low pay, etc.).

Contributing to the mix of challenges is an increasingly intense scrutiny from the media and general public. There's not a week that goes by when some magazine, newspaper, television program, website, blogger, or publication isn't professing how troubled public schools are. Unfortunately, the blunt of the scrutiny always falls on urban schools that serve poor and minority students.

At the center of all the scrutiny, controversy, and uncertainty is the urban school principal. This person is responsible for providing leadership in this tumultuous environment. The hours for the principal have become increasingly longer, and the stakes have also become higher.

The dynamics of the position (the role and duties, stakeholders, policies, procedures, authority, etc.) are constantly changing. Individuals who occupy this position must possess leadership qualities and the temperament to meet the extreme needs and diverse circumstances of the students, staff, and communities in which the schools are located.

The Hard Truth: Problems and Issues in Urban School Reform was written for two major reasons. First, it was designed to connect new and aspiring urban school principals to the realities of the position from a practitioner's viewpoint. This book brings to light many of the harsh issues affecting urban schools and the conditions that caused them.

While reading this book, new and aspiring principals will see urban school reform in relation to the real issues they will have to face while occupying an urban school principalship, which will give them greater insight and means for solving complex problems.

Second, experienced principals can use this book as a barometer to analyze and measure their own administrative practices and effectiveness. This book will validate what many experienced principals know to be true about urban schools while giving them a framework for making connections with their own school's environment in a genuine way.

Principals who can genuinely connect with their school's environment will be able to take negative situations within urban schools and forge them into positive outcomes. They will also be able to gain a better understanding of the politics associated with their respective school buildings, which will help them to make better informed decisions and improve their overall effectiveness as a school leader.

The issues plaguing urban schools and the methods mentioned in this book for addressing them are not commonly discussed in most school leadership textbooks with the same amount of candor and detail. I cover topics that many scholars shy away from or are oblivious to.

I have acquired a unique perspective that will take most scholars years to gain. As stated previously, I once lived in poverty and attended urban schools. While others write from the comfort of academia and offer their opinions on what they think would work, I talk about real situations and real solutions that principals can apply to their schools' unique circumstances, and I provide the reasoning behind such solutions.

A plethora of leadership books focus on the technical side of the principalship (graduation ceremonies, curriculum, policies and procedures, book distribution and materials, hiring staff, budget allocations, etc.), but schools are social institutions with varying degrees of complex networks. This book exposes many of the sociopolitical aspects of school leadership not commonly discussed, and it provides a framework for how principals can maneuver through such an environment to bring about effective change.

Some of the methods mentioned for achieving positive outcomes may be a little unconventional or even controversial. My hope is that the reader will have an open mind when digesting the content of this book because I don't spare any punches when delivering the Hard Truth. The chapters are raw and uncensored, and they touch the essence of what's really going on in today's urban schools.

It is my belief that every principal working in an urban school has a choice: she or he can coast by and maintain the status quo or actively work to make a difference in the quality of education being rendered to the largest population of disadvantaged students in America. My hope is that after reading the following chapters, principals will choice the latter.

Acknowledgments

First, I must give all praise and honor to YHWH: the creator of the heavens, earth, the sea, and all that there is. HE has given me the mental power and courage to stick with this endeavor, despite the many obstacles that I had to encounter along the way.

Second, I'd like to thank my immediate family: wife Tia, sons A'mon and Amiyr, daughter Aniyah, and my mother Jean. Collectively, they are my source of inspiration and the reasons for my labors.

I would also like to thank all of my professors at Miami University, professional mentors, and advisors for sharing their insights and allowing me the opportunity to learn from them. The knowledge that I've gained over the years will stay with me forever. My hope is that I will also be able to impart valuable educational leadership lessons to the next generation of educators in the same manner.

Last but not least, I want to acknowledge all of the dedicated educators, administrators, and support staff who work tirelessly on behalf of today's urban students. Students who attend urban schools truly need positive figures in their lives that will not only teach them but also care about them. They need educators who have the capacity to nurture, support, correct, and show them the value of a quality education. I truly understand the difficulties that come with working in most urban schools, so I applaud the efforts of urban school professionals and hope that they continue to make positive things happen for students.

Introduction

This book is designed to give firsthand knowledge of the variegated issue that affects the urban school principalship and school reform. The topics addressed expose many of the barriers that hinder the teaching and learning process and keep urban schools swimming in seas of failure. Although many of the issues presented in this book are common to all school principals, they are not commonly discussed in most graduate school administrative programs or leadership textbooks.

My goal is to bring these issues to the forefront so that current and aspiring school principals will gain a deeper understanding about the issues, people, and circumstances affecting urban schools. Having an in-depth understanding of the tough issues, school leaders will be equipped to handle them, therefore making the schools and the people within them better.

OVERVIEW OF CHAPTERS

Chapter 1 discusses the overall problems plaguing urban education and describes the principal's role within such an environment. It also defines the temperament and attitude that urban school principals must have to be effective in a tough school environment. This chapter also talks about how principals should deal with the bureaucracy, politics, mayhem, and sometimes dysfunction that often exist within urban schools districts.

After the first chapter, the remaining chapters follow a slightly different format. From the second chapter onward, I outline a particular problem or issue that plagues most urban schools; then, I use the second half of the chapter to discuss the Hard Truth, which also provides a framework that will help urban school principals resolve that particular issues.

For example, chapter 2 discusses how urban school principals should deal with conflict. The first half of the chapter outlines the most common types of conflict that most urban school principals experience and how those conflicts affect the overall functioning of the school and the morale of the school's staff. The latter half of the chapter discusses the uncensored truth about what principals really need to do to resolve all conflicts encountered.

Chapter 3 deals with a principal's ability to avoid entrapments from those in and around the school setting. This is vital to the principal's effectiveness and integrity as a school leader. Some people within the school setting attempt to use crafty devices to gain the principal's trust and confidence. Once they gain his or her confidence, they use it to push their agendas or practice a form of abuse that will be detrimental to the school's transformation at some level. I discuss what principals should and should not do when confronted by such people.

Chapter 4 talks about the importance of learning a school's culture and what should be done when the school's culture is a negative one. It also discusses avenues that principals can take to maintain the positive aspects while working to change the less desirable parts, without experiencing a lot of resistance or causing huge divisions among the stakeholders involved.

Parent engagement is a very important part of any school's success. While some parents work to support the schools their children attend, a large number of parents in urban schools don't. The number of parents that are angry, uncooperative, and present problems for school officials are growing with each passing year. Some even come to the school and display their dissatisfaction in inappropriate ways. Chapter 5 informs principals how to deal with irate parents and work with them to resolve their issues and problems.

Chapters 6–8 give a framework for dealing with stagnation, troublemakers on the staff, and disruptive students—all of which are prevalent factors in most urban schools today (especially those with a history of failure). A principal's inability to deal with such factors will have great consequences on the success of the school and her or his overall ability to provide leadership in an effective manner.

Chapters 9 and 10 both deal with improving student achievement, the measuring stick by which schools and principals are rated. These two chapters provide a framework for principals to follow, highlighting important factors that principals should focus on and pointing out specific behaviors that principals should do to monitor the school's progress.

The final chapters, 11–14, deal with a principal's ability to critique his or her own practice. This is important because it is a mechanism that principals can use to learn from their mistakes and successes. These chapters also discuss how principals should make time to personally reflect and think critically about interactions, programs, conversations, and events that happen within the school's environment.

America is currently at a turning point in its history with regard to public education. Urban school reform is a key factor in whether our country will move forward or lag behind other industrialized nations. The people who lead these schools and the decisions they make while occupying the principalship will have a lasting impact on the educational climate in this country for years to come.

ONE
The Leadership Void in Today's Urban Schools

Many factors play a huge part in why most urban schools in major U.S. cities are not performing well. Although there isn't one factor that can be attributed most of the blame, having an effective school leader serving as principal can greatly reduce (and in some cases eliminate) many of the problems.

Being an effective principal in an urban school district is easier said than done. The principalship is challenging in any school district, but principals who work in urban school districts face a host of obstacles that are unique and, at times, vastly different from those of principals who work in private, rural, suburban, or religious schools.

An urban school district is one that constitutes or encompasses a city or town whose schools are administered by a local school board located in a metropolitan area. The word *urban* normally serves as an alternate for words such as *inner city, central city, downtown, metropolitan, nonrural, ghetto, low socioeconomic status,* and *business district*. So when I use the term *urban schools*, I'm not referring to schools with students from middle-class or affluent families. I'm specifically talking about schools that service students who live in poverty or similar conditions.

The greatest difference between urban schools and their private, suburban, and rural counterparts is the high concentration of minority students that come from families of low socioeconomic status, meaning those who live near or below the poverty line. Students who come from families in poverty usually do not have the educational resources as students from middle-class or affluent families (additional books, computers and laptops, the Internet and other technology, additional tutoring, etc.), which becomes an impediment to the quality of education they receive.

Some rural districts may also have students of low socioeconomic status, but those students are usually more homogeneous, having the same ethnic background, community values, social norms, and language. Having a homogeneous student population is beneficial to school districts because it limits the number of barriers that stand in the way of teaching and learning—making it a lot easier for school officials to ascertain students' academic needs and deficiencies.

Most urban school districts, especially those in large metropolitan cities, have very diverse student populations, most of which also happen to live near or below the poverty line. The students who attend urban districts vary in race, income, social norms, beliefs, community supports, and sometimes language.

According to Howard, Dresser, and Denklee (2009), blacks, Hispanics, and children from a wide array of Asian and Middle Eastern cultures make up nearly half of students nationwide, and they are the dominant majority in many of the schools located in low-income neighborhoods. Although many outside the urban educational community might view this kind of diversity as a means for celebration, it can bring an array of learning and behavioral challenges for urban school districts to contend with when trying to provide the best educational experience for all students involved.

In addition to having to educate low-income students with an array of academic and cultural needs, urban schools principals are faced with high levels of student violence and disciplinary issues, low parental support, annual decreasing budgets, problems with attracting and retaining highly qualified teachers, low staff morale, continually low standardized test scores, and pressure from state and federal mandates (to name just a few).

To make matters worse, the principalship in general has been stripped of most of its power and authority. In many urban school districts, principals have been made to operate within a vacuum, therefore limiting the scope and range of their actions, but the decrease in authority has done little to minimize increases in responsibility and expectations. They are still expected to ensure that all students achieve at high levels despite their environmental circumstances and academic deficiencies.

The current factors mentioned so far have, in many ways, tied the hands of principals and placed limitations on what they can do. These restrictions have great implications: adversely affecting basic administrative functions such as hiring staff, making budget allocations, enforcing discipline codes and school policies, disciplining ineffective staff, and implementing needed schoolwide reforms.

The issues faced by urban school principals are compounded when they are required to share key school-based decisions with individuals whose interests are not aligned with the school's overall mission. Such individuals are often able to insert themselves into other areas of school management and operations traditionally designed for principals and other administrators.

Their insertion into key areas of school operations has given them an inflated (and sometimes distorted) view of their importance and overall position associated within the school. At their most powerful state, these individuals can influence the employment status of the principal (regardless of the principal's acumen and job performance).

I'm not advocating that principals should act alone when making vital decisions that will affect the school, students, staff, and the greater learning community, but too many unregulated voices in matters of importance will quickly lead to split decision making, confusion, and disorganization, which is the current state of many urban schools across America. When an organization suffers from split decision making, two things usually happen: (1) important issues don't progress as quickly as they should, because the group can't come to a consensus on what's important or which direction to proceed, and (2) certain individuals will base their decisions according to their self-interests instead of those that best serve the organization. The result is that students will ultimately suffer because their educational needs will go unmet.

The phenomenon just described has caused a wave of changes in the way that urban school principals view themselves and the work they are paid to perform. It's unfortunate, but many urban school principals have experienced longevity in their positions not because of any major improvements they've implemented, increases in student achievement they've effected, or any other vital area germane to school improvement they've influenced. Rather, many of them have been able to prolong their employment by one of two ways: by default or by maintaining friendly relationships with certain people.

Many urban schools are in such bad conditions and have such bad reputations that the pool of candidates who are willing to lead the schools out of failure is limited. An even larger portion of urban school principals have been able to last in their roles because they've been able to form and maintain relationships with the "right" people—meaning people with some perceived influence or clout.

These are the kinds of administrators who are desperately trying to please everyone, hoping it will lead to job security. They spend more time fraternizing than actually working on items of real importance. What was once a position of respect, honor, and prestige within the urban school/educational community has now been reduced to a pseudo-popularity contest in some cases.

Despite the growing number of urban school principals who fall in the aforementioned categories, there are still many talented, hardworking, and capable school leaders who are committed to improving their schools and the communities they serve. But the reality is that most effective principals in urban schools do not remain in their positions very long. Some move on to central office to occupy upper administrative positions, or they move on to more "desirable" schools in suburban or affluent school districts—usually within the first three to five years of accepting a principalship within an urban school.

Many good principals move from urban schools for various reasons, but one of the more prevalent reasons is that they use urban schools as stepping-stones to gain experience before moving on to the next position. It is a rare occurrence to see a successful principal reform an urban school and then remain in that same position over a prolonged period.

A principal who successfully reforms an ineffective urban school will quickly make a name for himself or herself within the surrounding educational community. He or she will either become sought after by affluent school districts or become enticed by the idea of being able to make more money in more suitable working conditions (nicer office, ample budget, highly qualified staff with high morale, diverse programs and activities for students, well-maintained school building, functional equipment, committed support staff, integrated technology, less student behavioral issues, etc.).

The belief is that if a principal can successfully reform a failing urban school, then he or she can do wonders in an affluent setting with more resources and support. This dynamic has caused many urban school districts to experience a lot of inconsistency and turnover in leadership because principals are coming and going at higher-than-average rates. I've known some urban schools to experience a change in leadership once every two years. In many instances, the only people who are having longevity are the ones who don't need to be in those positions.

The factors mentioned so far have caused a void in urban school leadership that's currently being filled, in too many instances, by the wrong types of individuals. Many such types who have been able to keep their jobs over time have fallen under the false notion that being liked by various stakeholder groups leads to job security and longevity. The intense desire to be liked and to please others has caused many urban school principals to become timid, soft, and too conservative—worrying too much about what others think about them and less about resolving real school issues.

Many urban school principals who have occupied their positions for an extended period tend to shy away from touchy issues and avoid confrontation at all cost. This is done out of fear of making someone upset; they fear that someone might write a letter, make a phone call and complain, file a grievance, talk bad about them to colleagues, or rant about their actions to someone in central office.

The timidity of urban school principals has also caused them to make decisions that are politically charged, based on friendships, collegial networks, and associations. Therefore, they neglect the needs of students, parents, teachers, and other school staff in the process. The result is that many of the decisions being made by urban school principals contribute to the overall ineffectiveness of their schools. For many urban schools, this mentality perpetuates the status quo of low performance and failure.

COURAGEOUS LEADERSHIP

To effectively deal with the various factors plaguing most urban schools, principals need to be COURAGEOUS when caring out their administrative duties and responsibilities. This is the foundation for all actions and decisions made while occupying an urban school principalship.

Courageous principals are risk takers, and they have the heart to confront tough issues because they are confident in themselves and their abilities. They don't try to avoid making hard decisions, nor are they ultraconservative. They don't rely on their relationships or friendly networks to sustain their employment; instead, they focus on getting results that move urban schools forward. Courageous principals have the strength to do the right thing, even when it's not popular.

Being courageous also means taking an active role in dealing with people and situations that adversely affect the school. Courageous principals can effectively deal with circumstances, events, and people because they are operating from a position of strength and self-confidence. They hold themselves and other people accountable, and they are not overly conscious about what others personally think about them.

Understand: the main objective for a principal working in a school in need of reforms is to improve the conditions of the school for students, parents, staff, and the greater community. This means that principals have to protect, defend, define, and establish a positive learning culture for the benefit of all those involved.

Administrators who act courageously do not panic when faced with rapid change or chaos. They can think in the moment and adapt to the current circumstances and issues surrounding them. They view tough circumstances as an opportunity to prove themselves and test their leadership abilities. Being courageous opens possibilities for urban school principals and sparks a positive momentum for moving urban schools in a positive direction.

Female principals must also approach their work from this courageous mind-set. Most female principals face additional scrutiny that often escapes male principals. For example, if female principals are perceived by others as being too nice, people will try to take advantage of them and disrespect their authority and leadership.

In contrast, if female principals don't display enough traditional "feminine" qualities and characteristics, people will say they are trying to overcompensate, or they will accuse them of being too stern and uncompromising. Acting courageously helps female principals transcend such meaningless constructs and helps them remain focused on creating positive outcomes for their schools.

The following excerpt is from Whitaker (2002), and it explains the importance of having an effective leader governing a school:

> Researchers since the 1970's have examined the differences between those schools defined as more effective and schools defined as less effective. One of the most consistent characteristics of an effective school is the existence of a strong and fearless leader.

Courageous leadership is based on the following premise: urban schools need leadership that is just as tough as the issues they will face. A principal plays a vital role in the overall functioning and success of any school. If the head of the school is weak, timid, ineffective, and afraid to deal with the tough issues, then the entire school will mirror the same characteristics. Courageous principals act on who they are, and they make decisions based on what they value about education.

Leadership is a necessary condition for effective reform relative to school-, teacher-, and student-level factors (Marzano, 2003). The type of leadership displayed from the principal position will either serve as the catalyst for change or contribute to what many schools experience as the status quo of failure and low performance.

The following chapters outline how and why urban school principals should be courageous. The chapters also contain real issues that affect the urban schools of today and the principals who lead them—highlighting methods and strategies for resolving tough issues using the courageous mind-set. Many of the issues discussed might be a bit controversial or unconventional in comparison to most educational leadership textbooks. Other books often have a milder, less direct approach to school leadership reform.

A gentler and more conventional approach to school reform doesn't blend with the current needs of most urban schools—especially ones with a history of failure and dysfunction. Most urban schools are in a crisis; therefore, they need crisis intervention. The time for unproductive traditional methods and philosophies has passed.

Now is the time to think outside the box and challenge old practices and ways of doing things. The school leaders of today must be ready and willing to step up to the plate and contend with the tough issues that adversely affect student achievement in urban schools. This book is a guide that urban school principals can use to deal with the complexities of urban schools and achieve success not just for themselves but for the schools and greater communities in which they serve.

TWO
Conflict and Friction

The success of a principal working in an urban school will largely depend on his or her ability to effectively deal with various forms of conflict. Due to the current state of urban schools, principals should expect conflict and friction on all fronts (from students, parents, staff members, the community, etc.). The various forms of conflict can mostly be attributed to some stakeholders having separate agendas, interests, and motives that are not directly in alignment with what's needed for the school's improvement.

In many urban schools, especially those with a history of failure, there are stakeholders who are selfish, self-centered, and only out to satisfy their personal needs. They could care less about the school's overall success or how their actions, interest, and decisions will affect the school's general functioning and progress. This is what usually happens when there are many people lobbing for various levels of control over a limited amount of resources.

Some of the conflict and friction will stem from aggressive types within the school's stakeholder groups. These people are usually bold, vociferous, and tactical and deliberate in their actions. They will make calls, send e-mails, and write letters to openly complain or criticize the principal and the school, and they will actively work to stir up confusion, controversy, strife, and dissention.

Other kinds of conflicts will come from more passive-aggressive types. These people can be more dangerous than their aggressive counterparts because they are harder to identify; they tend to be more covert with their actions. They will smile and laugh in the principal's face but will work behind the scenes to cause confusion and sow discord. They will also have the ability to use others to do their bidding while they sit back and watch.

To mask their true intentions, the passive-aggressive types will also try to stand behind some moral cause or some tradition that's entrenched in the hearts and minds of other stakeholders. Whichever is the case, it all boils down to each type trying to advance a particular agenda. These same groups could also try to form alliances with the principal, but if the principal doesn't cooperate, then he or she could experience various forms of conflict because of it.

Most urban school principals find it a little easier to handle student-related conflicts, but when it comes to dealing with adult-related issues from various stakeholders (staff, parents, community members, etc.), they fail miserably. The inability to effectively handle conflicts from stakeholders is mainly due to most principals' lack of training in this area while in graduate school.

It's no secret that most graduate school leadership programs are heavily based in philosophies associated with collaboration, democracy, and unity building. School leaders are mostly taught how to "get along." They spend more time studying ways of how to make everyone in the school "happy" instead of how to deal with conflicts associated with implementing change among the diversified needs of the stakeholder groups.

The graduate school training that most principals receive, combined with some principals' insatiable desire to be liked, has caused them to totally avoid confrontation and conflict. In most cases, they don't want to cause any waves because that goes against everything they were taught and believe in. When reflecting on my own graduate school experiences, I can remember being heavily indulged with school leadership principles that fostered being deferential, agreeable, and compromising to the point where conflicts were almost considered taboo.

I'm not advocating that principals shouldn't attempt to collaborate, practice democratic values, or promote unity among staff members. All are good characteristics that principals should practice when engaging others in the school setting. Operating in such a manner should be a principal's primary mode for interacting with stakeholders on all levels. But the avoidance of, or inability to effectively deal with, conflict will cause principals to delay necessary actions and decisions on issues that could greatly affect the school.

Two things usually happen as a result of a principal's inability or unwillingness to deal with conflicts: first, issues fester until they reach a boiling point and the principal is forced to respond, which will probably lead to an inappropriate response due to the delays in addressing the issues; second, the principal submits to the will of the person or group pushing the alternative school agenda. Either way, the principal looks bad and contributes to the ineffectiveness of the school.

THE HARD TRUTH

Urban school principals can't be so naïve to think that all stakeholder groups desire the same outcomes for the school as they do. Stakeholder groups are filled with people who do not have much invested in the school's overall success, so it's obvious why they may have ulterior motives or hidden agendas. Some may even have good intentions, but good intentions don't count on the school's state report card.

Understand: there will be some people from the various stakeholder groups who will genuinely want to assist and help the school move forward. The sincere individuals will not only have ideas about what the school needs but also be willing to put in the necessary work to bring the ideas to fruition. They're willing to volunteer their time, effort, and resources toward the benefit of the school. It would serve urban principals well to listen to the collective voices of these people and work in collaboration with them.

On the flip side, there are going to be those who, after listening to their ideas, will operate in a divisive manner unless their individual needs and interest are satisfied. When principals encounter people whose agendas and interests don't mesh with the school's overall mission, they must stop these people immediately. This means confronting the person or issue by taking necessary actions or making a stern decision.

Doing so will immediately declare the principal's position on the issue, which will either encourage or discourage further actions from others. If a person or group tries to proceed in a direction contrary to the school's overall mission, then the principal must use all of his or her intellectual and physical resources to stop their advancement—plain and simple. Multiple voices in a choir only sound good if they are in harmony with one another.

Avoiding conflicts within the school doesn't help matters; it only makes matters worse—it encourages others to go further. They will take as much as they can until the principal loses control, authority, and respect in some cases. By confronting an issue directly, principals not only declare their position but also let people know that there are some lines that can't be crossed. Principals should normally practice democratic values, but when certain boundaries are crossed, they must instantly switch over to a more direct and aggressive stance.

Courageous principals are not afraid to cause waves if it means protecting some aspect of the school or holding others accountable for their actions or duties. In fact, a principal working in an urban school with a history of failure should cause waves to ripple throughout the school at various points throughout the school year. The waves represent effective changes, initiatives, and practices that the school needs for advancement.

The Process for Resolving Conflicts

There is a process for successfully handling conflicts within the school setting. Principals cannot control the person's behavior that they are confronting, but they can control their own. When confronted about a particular issue, some people might behave inappropriately or act pretentiously. The following points provide a framework for addressing individuals and achieving the most desirable outcomes.

Always remain calm. Principals should never get into a shouting match with any person within the school setting. Even if the other person is upset and acting inappropriately, the principal should always keep her or his cool and emotions intact; a principal should never respond with the same level of aggression as the other person. The principal must maintain one's integrity at all times. When people behave unruly, it usually means that they're out of control, unstable, or not in a comfortable position. When principals identify that they're dealing with someone who lacks self-control, they should automatically assume the dominant position and take the higher road. In fact, principals should always answer irate behavior with demure responses.

Clearly describe the issue. When confronting an individual, principals should never stray from the overarching problem or allow themselves to be lead astray. The person being confronted might try to steer the principal off course by bringing up nonrelated issues, making excuses for their shortcomings, pointing out issues with other people, or blaming the principal. They will try to bring up any tangential issue they can think of to take the glare off themselves. Principals must remain steadfast and not be swayed. They must communicate the issues clearly and concisely and remain free of ambiguity.

Listen to the other person. Being a good listener is very important when dealing with conflict. Oftentimes, both parties want to be heard, so no one is listening to what the other is saying. As the school's leader, the principal must actively listen to the other person's point of view. In listening, principals might be able to uncover the causes of the conflict or determine the best possible action for resolving the issue. It is not unusual for principals to learn that the other person didn't know their actions or behavior was causing a problem. Bringing the issue to the forefront can help one understand her or his fallacy. Being a good listener is paramount for principals when conversing about critical issues.

Clearly express the desired behavior or outcome. After the issue has been clearly defined, the next step is to define the desired behavior or outcome. This too should be explained clearly and concisely. It should be free of ambiguity so the other person clearly understands the expectations. This part of the conversation is typically when the other person will start bringing up past accomplishments or anything to make him or her look less problematic. Principals can't allow themselves to be swayed by this. They must stick to the point, reiterate the outcomes they want to see, and confirm the person's understanding of such outcomes.

Follow the conversation with documentation. After the meeting, the principal should write a brief memo to the other person, outlining the key points of the conversation. This is a good practice for several reasons. First, it reinforces the points discussed during the meeting, putting further emphasis on the seriousness of the problem. Second, if the person's actions or behavior persists, then the memos will serve as the necessary documentation to proceed toward the next level of progressive discipline.

Does being courageous mean that principals should never collaborate, compromise, or try to please others? Absolutely not! There are times when collaboration, compromise, and pleasing others is what's needed for a particular situation. There will even be times when principals should delegate and let others take the lead on certain issues and matters.

Understand: confronting problems and dealing with conflict is a good way to achieve growth. Some of the best innovations, discoveries, and advances in life have come out of conflicts being resolved. Conflict is not something that principals should view as being taboo or avoided at all cost within the school setting.

When principals avoid conflict, they give off the impression that they're afraid to deal with certain issues, circumstances, or people who are causing problems. Avoidance is a sign of weakness to some, and when they perceive a weakness, they will attack and never let up. Urban schools need leaders that are not afraid to deal with conflicts. It will ultimately lead to the school's growth and progression.

THREE
Individual Entrapments

The principal is the most sought-after person within the school building. This position ranks second to only the school district's superintendent with regard to the amount of attention and controversy the position attracts. Students, teachers, parents, community representatives, central office staff, and a host of other stakeholders all want part of the principal's time, attention, and/or support.

By virtue of the authority given to the principal, many people will seek to gain his or her confidence by using a variety of tactics. Some individuals want the principal's support for genuine reasons that will benefit the school, while others want it for reasons that are not genuine.

Some of the more common tactics used to gain the principal's support are as follows: using various forms of flattery, being overly complimentary, expressing personal hardships to gain sympathy, overly displaying support for the principal's ideas, divulging personal information, and complaining about the effectiveness of other employees. There are some who like to distract the principal with banal conversation at odd moments in the school day.

But the most frequently used tactic of them all is that of offering to buy the principal lunch or perform personal favors. I refer to these tactics and others like them as *individual entrapments*. I've heard of situations when principals have allowed staff members to pick up their dry cleaning, wash their cars, do work around their homes, fix their personal computers, and even babysit their children—all done out of the "goodness" of the persons' hearts, of course.

All principals must understand that there is no such thing as a free ride. Everything has a price tag (especially if done undercover by someone within the school setting). Any personal favors or deeds done for the principal with "no strings attached" are truly done with underlying motives.

Whether the parties admit it or not, their motives are to gain the principal's trust or confidence and/or involve the principal in some emotional entanglement. Once principals are caught in these kinds of situations, they tend to judge individuals less by their job performance and more by the favors performed outside the employee's true job description.

It's no coincidence that the individuals who are offering to do the favors are typically the ones with issues surrounding low performance, stagnation, neglect, incompetence, or inefficiency. Individual entrapments are dangerous for principals and detrimental to the school as a whole because they cloud the principal's judgment and blind his or her eyes from seeing the true nature of a person or the full scope of a situation.

This is one of the reasons why some ineffective people and programs within urban schools stay longer than they should. Principals grow to like, depend, or feel comfortable with or obligated to certain individuals for reasons outside their normal job duties. These employees' inefficiency and weaknesses are overlooked due to their personal ties with the principal. Such unhealthy and unproductive relationships also stand in the way of the school's acquiring competent individuals who can perform tasks effectively.

For example, I know of a situation when a principal became a victim to one of the simplest of entrapments. The principal was head of a high school of 660 students with 55 staff members. The principal agreed to let one of the staff members, an English teacher, buy refreshments with her own money for the entire staff during a professional development session. Initially, the principal said no, but the teacher was persistent. The teacher said it would be her pleasure to do it, so the principal conceded.

The refreshments were a big hit with the staff because they typically were not fed during professional development sessions. After a long day of work, the refreshments seem to give the teachers a bit of a spark during the session, which lasted two hours after the regular school day. After the session ended, the teacher informed the principal that she would provide refreshments for the next meeting as well. The principal also agreed.

The teacher continued to do this "voluntarily" for each professional development session held throughout the school year. Each time there was a session after school, the food became even more elaborate. The teacher started out with providing basic snacks, but it eventually led to full-course meals with dessert.

Throughout the school year, one of the counselors noticed that many students were asking to be removed from one particular teacher's English classes. It was the English teacher who provided the food for the professional development meetings. Students complained about the teacher being mean, rude, and unwilling to explain the lessons to their understanding. The students also said the teacher merely passed out worksheets and sat behind her desk—that is, whenever she was not yelling or talking down to them.

The counselor shared this information with the principal. She also informed the principal of how frequent these kinds of situations happen with this particular teacher. She further reported that every semester, students come to her office in droves asking to be removed from this teacher's classroom. Several parents also raised complaints. As a result, the teacher's classes were reduced to 8 to 10 students, while other English teachers' classes became overloaded.

After receiving the information from the counselor, the principal also realized that a large number of students who came to the office with disciplinary referrals were sent by the same English teacher. Instead of investigating the matter or conversing with the teacher about the issues, the principal decided to do nothing. The principal neither confronted the teacher nor attempted to deal with the issues, because he feared that the teacher might become offended, which could prompt her to stop buying food for the professional development sessions. Instead, he avoided the issue and allowed the problem to continue.

THE HARD TRUTH

The aforementioned example is a good demonstration of why principals should never become entangled in the favors and false niceties of employees on the staff. Principals must ask themselves the following questions when confronted with a seemingly sincere gift or favor: Why is this person offering this to me or the school? What does this person have to gain by offering this gesture of kindness? What do I or the school stand to lose by accepting this gift or favor? Will accepting this gift compromise my integrity or authority, or will it cloud my judgment as the school's leader?

Principals must also operate pragmatically: judging people, events, and programs based on the results they produce. People who are truly about the business of teaching and learning don't have time to waste cajoling or being chummy with the principal. All their time is devoted to creating positive outcomes for students.

When principals fall victim to entrapments, they put themselves in positions where they can't act courageously. If they feel indebted to someone for reasons not beneficial to the school's progress, then they will not be able to stand strong and act courageously when needed, nor will they be able to make the right decision when doing so might be unpopular.

Urban school principals should avoid accepting personal favors and freebies at all costs, because they usually come with a hidden price tag. Courageous principals have the nerve to say no to both. They will not allow themselves to fall prey and become entrapped by such false acts of kindness, which will lead only to their own ineffectiveness.

It takes courage to say no, even if it might momentarily hurt someone's feelings. It's better for principals to hurt someone's feelings than have to compromise their integrity in the long run. Avoiding entrapments allows principals to operate freely and independently; they won't feel obligated, nor will they feel the need to succumb to those who are trying to skate by without producing positive results. They can talk straight with people and take bold action when necessary.

Principals who are not entangled are free to question, critique, monitor, reprimand, and evaluate without fear of anything or anyone. The moment that urban school principals become entangled with emotional attachments or bonded by personal favors, they will undoubtedly become less authoritative, less assertive, and less critical of the people, programs, and behaviors that happen in and around the school.

Two final points: there are a few times when it is okay to accept a gift, favor, or present. Celebrations such as National Boss's Day, holiday gatherings where gifts are exchanged (when random names are selected for gift giving), or end-of-the-year gifts of appreciation from the entire staff are acceptable. These kinds of gifts are fine because they're more associated with building community within the school and not solely about the principal. Any gift given in secret or any favors done simply by virtue of your position should be turned down completely.

Lastly, there may be times when people gain the principal's trust and confidence in the correct manner, but a situation might arise when the staff member behaves inappropriately. Maybe she or he missed a deadline, started abusing a policy, or neglected to follow certain procedures. Whatever the case might be, principals must be able to act courageously and deal with the situation. They can't let the employee's past performance and deeds affect their judgment. Principals have to be consistent and fair with their correction no matter who's receiving it.

FOUR
School Culture

Many principals, especially novice ones, make the mistake of underestimating the significance that culture has on all aspects of the school. A positive school culture can foster high morale, collaboration, high staff performance, and high student achievement. A negative school culture can lead to low morale, disunity, disorganization, and poor performance on all levels. A school's culture can be compared to the blood of a living organism. Without the blood, there is no life.

There are many leadership philosophies that discuss facilitating a positive school culture, but few give details as to how to work within a school's negative cultural conditions. Every school has its own culture, norms, and patterns of behavior that have been accepted and perpetuated for years. In many urban schools that have a history of failure, the cultural norms could be mostly negative, but they are so engrained in the minds and behavior of the stakeholders that it will take a catastrophic event for any real change to occur.

One of the main reasons why the needed change is slow or why it never happens in many urban schools is because many principals fail to develop a keen understanding of the school's culture before they attempt to change it. They come into the school's environment with their own ideas of what will work or what the stakeholders (students, parents, community members, etc.) desire. Usually, their ideas stem from those they've implemented in other schools or things they've read about or heard other principals do.

What works in one urban school may have contrasting results in others. Due to the adverse environmental conditions associated in the communities where many urban schools are located and the various nuances that make each neighborhood distinct, urban schools have become very complex institutions. When principals try to operate without first knowing the school's culture, they put themselves at a great disadvantage.

Trying to operate within a school system without first understanding the existing culture is like trying to throw darts in the dark. You might get lucky and a few of the darts might hit the board, but the majority of them will be off, and even if you hit the board, the darts that land may not have much value. Principals who lack knowledge of school culture will make unnecessary mistakes when addressing issues, or they will be oblivious to the factors that most affect the school. If the negative aspects of a school's culture go unaddressed, almost all efforts of school reform will be pointless.

THE HARD TRUTH

Upon accepting the position, an urban school principal must have sound knowledge of the school's culture. A good understanding of the culture is not restricted knowledge of knowing who does what in the school; it involves extensive knowledge that speaks of shared beliefs and acceptable ways of behavior.

Principals must learn the school's history, traditions, celebrations, norms, heroes and heroines, statistics (graduation rates, student attendance, staff attendance, discipline referrals, and suspensions), staff morale, types of school programs and how they function, employee retention rates, and past awards and accomplishments, just to name a few. Having a keen understanding of a school's culture could serve as the principal's gateway to understanding and solving problems within the school.

Experienced and novice principals both make the mistake of being too self-absorbed when trying to understand a school's culture. They view it from their own perspective, which is a mistake. They have preconceived ideas about what they want to implement and establish without having any preliminary knowledge about the school and its stakeholders. Some of the veteran school principals may even be in denial about the true nature of their school's culture. Instead of dealing with the current circumstances, they are intent with riding on past perceptions or traditions, which may not be altogether accurate.

Principals must have the courage to step outside themselves and honestly view their school's culture for what it truly is at the current moment. They must look at the school's culture from the students, staff members, and other stakeholders' perspectives and not from a leadership standpoint. This will help principals to clearly see the gaps, problematic issues, and disconnected parts that need the most attention.

In addition to knowing the school's culture, principals need to become familiar with the communities in which the students live. According to

Wiles and Bondi (1998), in gathering information about the people who live in the area served by the school district, principals should attempt to understand the educational and cultural levels of the community, their general attitudes about the schools, and their expectations for education in the area.

Neighborhood schools and their communities are connected like a mother is to her child. It is a bond that's not easily broken. Many people would like to separate school operations from its community, but that sort of thinking is as much foolish as it is impossible; schools are an extension of the communities where they're located. The more principals learn about the communities where students come from—the norms, nuances, and acceptable ways of behavior—the more they'll learn about the students, their parents, and the school as a whole. This will allow them to make a deeper connection and help to ensure that the reforms and initiatives implemented will truly make a difference.

Gathering Information

One could gather community information in many ways: viewing public records and statistics, reading newspapers, or using the Internet. But for principals, the most effective way of gathering community information is to actually visit the communities themselves. Observing the communities firsthand is the best way for principals to put their fingers on the heartbeat of the people in the community.

When visiting neighborhoods where students live, principals should drive by and observe the conditions of the buildings, housing, and overall condition of the environment. They should also get out of their cars, walk around, and go inside a few establishments and strike conversations with people. The goal is to try to see the community through the lens of the residents. When speaking with people in the community, principals should ask questions about the school. Principals should try to talk to different people and gather as much information as possible by listening. This will give the principal insight on how the community views the school.

Principals can also host community-sponsored events or collaborate with grassroots organizations. I know of a middle school principal who allowed a local community watch group to use a classroom in the school building to host its biweekly meetings. To show its gratitude, the group helped to raise money to buy new uniforms for the school's volleyball team.

Personal interactions and engagement with the right members in the community can yield unbelievable returns. Visiting the communities will give principals a visceral connection with the school's overall landscape and serve as the mold for shaping future decisions and actions.

The effort that principals have to exert to learn a school's culture is courageous work because it forces the principal to move from behind his or her title and try to view the school's environment in the way that others see it. Some principals may not want to do that because they are afraid to open themselves to criticism or because the reality of their school's culture might not mesh with the ideas they have in their heads.

The unfortunate part is that their distorted and unrealistic view of their school's culture will be one of the main reasons why they can't lead the school out of its poor performing state. Due to their inability to recognize the real problems, their actions will never be sufficient for corrective measures and true reform.

Second, some principals might not want to be in a position where they're perceived as not knowing something. Being in this position makes some principals feel vulnerable, inferior, or unbecoming of a school leader. The reality is that principals are not expected to know everything at all times.

Asking questions and acknowledging when you don't know something makes you look more human and relatable to others. It's okay to tell people you will get back to them when you don't have an answer. Furthermore, finding the correct answers to questions helps principals expand their knowledge and grow professionally, which makes them more effective leaders in the long run.

Last, there will be times when urban school principals will have to confront negative cultural norms that have been entrenched in the hearts and minds of the stakeholders for generations. It will take a lot of courage to deal with such issues, but having a thorough understanding of the existing culture will help to inform decision making during such tough times and provide insight on what to say and do.

Knowledge of the school's culture will lend itself to figuring out who to call on for support, and it will indicate the best times to take action (or no action at all). This knowledge will also help principals to properly communicate the issues in ways that all stakeholders can understand and to convey the right messages so that the stakeholders are better able to accept the changes implemented.

Understanding a school's culture is the best way for principals to connect with the stakeholders. Principals who are able to create constructs that resonate with stakeholders can change negative cultural norms and move things forward more quickly. A principal's lack of knowledge about a school's exiting culture is detrimental not only to the school but also to his or her effectiveness as a leader. The only way to change an institution and its negative cultural norms is to first learn everything there is to know about it.

FIVE
Irate Parents

One of the most challenging aspects to educators and to school leaders on all levels is having to deal with is difficult or irate parents. Out of all the tasks that school officials have to contend with, dealing with parents who are rude, disrespectful, or overly aggressive is probably the most dreaded.

Many urban educators are uncomfortable with interacting with irate parents. They feel intimidated, caught off guard, and at times insecure because they don't know how to deal with the parents' behavior. Some parents can be so imposing that they have the ability to make education professionals question their own abilities and actions. Most of the uneasiness in having to deal with irate parents comes from teachers and administrators because they're the ones who have to interact with them the most.

Over the course of my career in urban education, I've seen and experienced many bizarre situations involving irate parents. I've known some parents to call the school and use profane language toward anyone who answers the phone. Some have come to the school and threatened students and school employees with physical harm. I've even witnessed some parents behave so inappropriately that the police had to be called to remove them from the school's premises.

It's no coincidence that the parents who behave inappropriately are the same ones who will not return a phone call from a teacher, attend a parent-teacher conference, volunteer their time, or participate in their child's educational development in any manner; but if the principal is not able to see them on a day when they randomly appear at the school, they will raise all kinds of ruckus.

Many parents take an adversarial stance toward the urban schools where they send their children to be educated, which is not only counterproductive but also a symptom of a larger problem shared by the majority of urban schools: a lack of parental engagement.

Parents of urban school-age children typically do not volunteer at the school, advocate on the school's behalf, write letters expressing their concerns, or raise funds for the school on any significant scale, nor do they frequently participate on any decision-making committees. The parents who do participate consistently in the aforementioned activities in urban schools are rare.

It's unfortunate, but the majority of parents of urban school-age children are usually seen at the school during entertainment events or fun activities (sports activities, talent shows, proms and homecomings, parades, holiday assembles, graduations, etc.) or if there is some major problem where their participation is mandatory (e.g., their child is being suspended or expelled from school), if they're seen at all.

This is not a gross generalization or stereotype but the truth. Take any urban school district in American and visit the school during a sporting event. There will be plenty of parents there, but visit the same school during a PTA meeting. Those same parents who attended the sporting events will be noticeably absent.

Despite the challenges that difficult/irate parents present, urban school principals must be able to interact with them effectively. Failure to do so can create a school culture that's apprehensive, fearful, or even unwilling to engage the parent population.

THE HARD TRUTH

To effectively deal with irate parents, urban school principals must understand the basic reasons that cause parents to behave in such a manner. Reason No. 1: many urban schools are not the most inviting places for parents. For example, the front office is usually the first stop for parents when entering the school building. It is the one place in the school building that represents the school the most. The impression that people receive from a school's front office will often influence their views and opinions about the school when they leave.

It's not uncommon to find front office staff members in many urban schools to be rude, unfriendly, and unapproachable to most visitors. Therefore, when parents visit the main office, they're not greeted politely. Instead of treating parents and visitors with respect, front office staff treat them as if they are a burden and unwelcomed in the school.

Reason No. 2: some urban schools are so dysfunctional and unorganized that they themselves cause many of the issues with parents. It is a common practice for urban school administrators and teachers to schedule meetings with parents during the day, only to have them wait two or three hours before being seen. Such actions send the signal to parents that the school doesn't respect their time or importance as parents. If a meeting with a parent must be scheduled during the school day, then the least that school officials can do is start and end the meeting in a timely fashion.

A single mother with multiple children, working two jobs, will become very upset if she is left waiting two hours after the original time of her scheduled appointment. She probably had to take off work to attend the meeting, so it's a strong possibility that her job is not going to pay her for the time she's away. The money she's losing while at the school could adversely affect her ability to maintain her household.

Looking into reasons that cause parents to become irate is really courageous work for urban school principals. It causes them to recognize factors where they or the school could act differently. When parents behave irately, most principals and school officials tend to shy away from the parents or avoid them altogether. In some of the worse cases, this mentality translates into a physical isolation of the parent population. Parents can sense the disconnection, which makes it easier for them to disassociate themselves from the school on various levels or display their dissatisfaction inappropriately.

Instead of avoiding irate parents, principals should attempt to engage them. Whenever a principal is confronted with an irate parent, the main thing to remember is to remain calm. Principals should never display the same level of anger and emotion that the irate parent is displaying. Just because the parent is talking loudly or using inappropriate language doesn't mean that the principal should do the same.

Principals can't control the actions of parents, but they can control their own. Answering parents with the same level of aggression will only enflame them more, which will lead to more inappropriate behaviors from both the parents and the principal.

Whenever a principal is confronted by an angry parent, he or she should first try to isolate the parent from onlookers or remove him or her from the hostile environment. The best place is the principal's office or some quiet area in the school building where the principal and the parent can discuss the issue. Isolation is the first step because it removes the parent from the heat of the moment and takes away the audience, which could inflame the situation.

An audience has a way of enhancing emotionally charged situations, making them appear to be more serious and volatile than what they really are. An audience also has a way of pushing the enflamed individual to go further with one's antics. For example, if a parent starts ranting in the front office about a particular issue in front of an audience of other parents and visitors, he or she will be more inclined to keep up an angry image, whether wrong or not.

The parent may truly be upset at the moment he or she lashed out, but if the principal tries to engage the parent in front of a crowd and expose where the parent may have been negligent, then it's very likely that the parent will try to find a way to be right instead of acknowledge where he or she may have been wrong. But if the parent were isolated from the audience, he or she would be more willing to calm down and be open to listening to what the principal has to say.

Successfully removing the parent from the hostile environment and the audience is half the battle. The next step is for principals to be good listeners. In most situations involving irate parents, their behavior for that moment was triggered due to an accumulation of previous bad experiences with the school or the school district. They've had issues with former principals and teachers or problems with other children.

In some cases, they're just fed up with the overall school system, so when they come to the school for the smallest of issues, they're usually geared up for combat. Many parents don't trust the school or school district because they've been made to feel systematically locked out of the decision-making process regarding their children's educational experiences and development.

This perception may not be altogether true in some cases; it is merely part of the larger problems that many parents have with other aspects of society. In most instances, these parents represent the families of low socioeconomic status. Such families live in some of the worst neighborhoods and communities, plagued by gang and domestic violence, drug addiction and abuse, crime, unemployment, and subpar housing and health care. The people of these communities generally distrust "systems" (political, law enforcement, etc.) because they either don't understand them or don't believe they will work on their behalf. In their minds, the educational system is no different.

Most of the parents of urban school-age children believe school officials generally don't care about what they think and do not want their input. Parents in such a mind-set may even believe that acting out is a way for them to be heard and to avoid being taken advantage of by school officials or the school district. When parents are in this state, the very least of things can cause them to explode.

This is why being a good listener is so important. Some parents just want to feel as though they're being heard. Many parents are not comfortable with writing letters or serving on committees, but they can express their feelings and opinions if someone takes the time to listen. Some parents merely want to vent their overall frustrations—most of which may not necessarily have anything to do with how the school is currently being operated, but it's good for the principal to listen anyway.

While conversing with parents, principals must be mindful not to raise their voices—even if the parent is talking loudly. When dealing with someone who is angry or acting irate, principals should always respond as if they are having a pleasant conversation with a good friend—regardless of the parent's behavior. A calm tone and demeanor has a way of taking all the aggression out of the irate person.

It is hard for some people to remain calm while another person is yelling at them or behaving in an aggressive manner, because it's a natural impulse to meet aggression with aggression or to flee from an aggressive individual. Despite the difficulty, principals must remain calm and respond appropriately, regardless of how the other person is acting. Principals will discover that in most cases, answering with a quiet tone will adjust the parent's temperament and bring one down to an appropriate level for effective dialogue, which leads to resolving the parent's issue and further building trust and establishing rapport. When listening, principals should do a lot of paraphrasing to ensure they clearly understand what the parent is trying to say. Trust and rapport building is the key. Once the principal has gained the parent's trust, the adversarial relationship between the school and the parent will cease.

Parental engagement is similar to student engagement. School leaders must make a genuine attempt to get to know the parents and understand them (Whitaker & Fiore, 2001). Urban school principals must find out parents' interests, concerns, questions, frustrations, and issues that affect them the most regarding the school and their children's place in it. There are multiply ways to acquire this information (surveys, conversations, meetings, home and community visits, etc.).

To get a clear assessment of what parents of urban school-age students truly expect out of the educational system, principals might have to venture out of the confines of the school building and reach out to parents in some nonconventional ways. I know a former urban school principal who once passed out a survey in a local tavern to elicit feedback from parents. Another principal went to the community bingo game held at 8 pm on a Friday night to reach out to the school's parent population.

The best method of reaching out to parents is directly related to the community and environmental conditions of the school. The strategies mentioned in chapters 2, 4, and 7 will greatly assist urban school principals in dealing with irate parents, by providing the background information that will help to inform decision making.

When parents see the principal going through great lengths to make them feel included, they will respond in positive ways. Even if there come times when parents might not see eye to eye with the school on an issue, the odds are that parents will not behave inappropriately because of the relationship that the principal has worked to cultivate.

After gaining a keen understanding of the issues and factors that affect parents, principals can move toward developing a strategic plan for engaging parents effectively. Notice how I continue to use the word *engagement* instead of the word *involvement*—because there is truly a difference. According to *Webster's*, the word *involvement* means "to affect or include." The same dictionary defines the word *engagement* as "to mesh, intermingle, or bind together as in a promise."

I thought it was necessary to highlight the difference in the two words because many educators and scholars use them interchangeably, but in actuality, they have different meanings in relation to urban schools. When schools involve parents, they usually lead with the school's interest in mind; but when schools attempt to engage parents, they lead with the parents' interests at the forefront (Ferlazzo & Hammond, 2009). Engagement fosters genuine collaboration and shared interest, while parental involvement merely encourages minimal participation.

Some urban school principals view questions, concerns, and issues from parents as a personal affront to their leadership. Others are self-serving of parents—only wanting to use them for their personal needs (bake sales, volunteering, conferences, additional resources, etc.), never addressing parents' needs or concerns in relation to the school's policies and practices. They don't view the parents as partners in the educational process. Such an attitude is counterproductive and doesn't get at the heart of true effective parental engagement.

Parental Engagement

An effective parental engagement plan is relative to the parents and schools being served. What works to engage parents in one urban school may not yield the same results in another. A school's parental engagement plan should outline ways in which parents can work with the school and not merely for the school.

This is a task that the principal should not undertake alone. It is a collaborative effort. Input should be gathered from parents, teachers, students, and other stakeholders. The plan should also include clearly defined objectives. The development and implementation of an effective parental engagement plan is one of the best forms of positive school change for any urban school.

According to Whitaker and Fiore (2001), the following are considered keys to successful parental engagement programs. Although the list is not an exhaustive one, it can be used as a basis for strategically developing an effective parental engagement plan.

- Assess families' needs and interests about ways of working with the school.
- Set clear and measurable objectives based on parent and community input.
- Hire and train a parent/family liaison to directly contact parents and coordinate activities.
- Develop multiple outreach mechanisms to inform families about policies and programs.

- Use creative forms of communication between educators and families.
- Provide staff development for teachers and administrators to enable them to work effectively with families and with each other in the educational process.
- Schedule programs and activities flexibly to reach diverse family groups.
- Evaluate the effectiveness of family engagement programs on a continual basis.

Many urban schools need to do more than routine contrived ways of fostering parental engagement (bake sales, open houses, required scheduled meetings by the district, etc.). I'm not saying that events such as bake sales and open houses should be abandoned, but there should be more to make the interactions between parents and the school meaningful. For example, during most open houses or back-to-school nights, parents have to endure the same routine of listening to the principals and teachers go over rules, policies, and procedures. Informing parents of such items is important, but there should be more depth to the presentations.

The interactions between the parents and the school need to be authentic and meaningful. Parents need to be equal participants and allowed opportunities for real contact, dialogue, constructive criticism, and negotiation. Most parents, regardless of their economic status or social class, want the best for their children, and they care about the quality of the education their children receive. It is the urban school principal's job to create structures that foster true parental engagement. This is the best way to reduce the number of irate parents encountered.

It goes back to understanding and building the school's culture. Principals who are able to genuinely connect with parents will get the best results from them. Schools and parents must work together to maximize the educational experience for students. Educators should never try to leave parents out of the equation or let the actions of a few dictate how the majority are treated within the school setting. School officials should view parents as the most important component to making the school a success.

One final note about dealing with irate parents: there are some parents who will behave inappropriately no matter how the school seeks to engage them. They have a personal ax to grind that probably stems from some issue in their childhood or some distant incident in their lives that can be helped only by intense therapy or psychiatric treatment.

If any parent crosses the line by displaying behaviors associated with or similar to making death threats on school staff, attempting physical harm on someone in the building, vandalizing school property, using excessive profanity or racial slurs, or stalking a student or school employee, the proper authorities (i.e., the police) should be contacted, and that parent should be barred from entering the school building indefinitely.

SIX

Troublemakers on the Staff

When effective principals start to make needed changes and reforms within the school, an interesting conundrum will start to take shape. Half of the stakeholders affected by the new reforms will love and applaud the much-needed changes, while the other half will hate the changes and the principal for implementing them.

The unsatisfied will moan, complain, gripe, and talk about how much better things used to be, even though student achievement was low and the overall functioning of the school was in disarray. I call these individuals *antagonists toward change*.

In some extreme cases, the antagonists will do whatever is in their power to negate the reform efforts because they benefited from the previous manner in which the school operated. Some might ask, how do some school employees benefit when the school is failing or performing at a subpar level? The truth is that some employees gain certain personal benefits while a school is not functioning properly.

Some school employees benefit from the status quo of failure because they can come to work late or leave early without repercussions, misappropriate school funds, misuse equipment, give subpar effort, or obtain special positions of prestige and power. Others may have held special affections for the former principal, which gave them special privileges and access within the school. Whatever the reason, these people will resent the changes no matter how good they are for the school overall.

It goes back to the precepts mentioned in chapter 2 about some stakeholders having alternative agendas. The ones who rebel against the school's needed improvements are mostly thinking of their own self-interests. They have trouble dealing with and accepting change no matter how menial.

If the reforms allow them to continue to operate in the manner in which they've grown accustom, no one will hear from them. Some may not necessarily object to the school's overall improvements; they'd just rather not have to do anything different in the process. In short, they want change to take place, but they don't want to change.

The antagonists' behavior is merely indicative of the school's overall climate. These employees did whatever they wanted simply because the school's climate or culture made it easy for them to do so and the principal allowed such behavior to take place. They took advantage of the system because no one monitored their actions or followed through with any real consequences.

Just like with any organization, only the truly dedicated and committed will perform their duties in a satisfactory manner without some authoritative figure standing over them—schools are no different. The antagonists toward change will try to take advantage of a situation to suit their individual desires, and they will continue to do so until someone has the courage to create conditions that will force them to change—the principal should serve as that person.

Urban school principals can't allow antagonists to poison reform efforts and perpetuate a status quo of failure. Occasional slippages or negligence by school-level employees could have great implications on many aspects of school operations: instruction, student achievement, best practices, and the overall functioning and efficiency. Urban school principals must work to maintain a positive school culture that's student centered and results driven. This will help to control or eliminate the damage that antagonists do.

THE DIEHARD REFORM ANTAGONIST

Once the school's administration establishes a positive culture that fosters consistency, organization, and efficiency, a large portion of the antagonists toward change will automatically follow suit because the school's culture will demand it of them. Those who are not aligned with the new climate will stick out like a sore thumb, and the pressure alone from their peers will be enough to keep them in line without the principal's ever having to say one word to them. The individuals with whom principals really need to be most concerned are the diehard reform antagonists; they are the real troublemakers.

The diehard reform antagonists are usually a small group of individual troublemakers who stand the most to lose from the changes that take place within the school. Before the changes, they had some perceived importance, held a prestigious title, received incentives or bonuses for doing relatively nothing, and were able to operate with impunity throughout the school building.

Due to the power and authority that their colleagues bestowed on them and the lack of administrative supervision, they were able to convince people and sway opinions, therefore giving them a high degree of personal and professional influence. Since the improvements threaten their influence in the workplace, they will not be happy with the changes.

They will harbor resentment, work to undo all the positive changes implemented, and attempt to stop any from occurring in the future. These types will use all their influence to maintain their status, even at the expense of the students and the school. If left alone, they will sow discord, stir up anxieties, infect others with negativity, divide the school into fractions, and wreak utter havoc throughout the building.

Before the school administration realizes what has happened, the reform efforts will appear ineffective and dissatisfaction will spread, leaving the principal baffled and confused. In some of the more extreme situations, the diehard antagonists use their power and influence to remove the principal from his or her position.

THE HARD TRUTH

When dissention and trouble spread among a school's staff, the principal often views it as coming from multiple sources and angles. But in actuality, most of the trouble can be linked to one dominant individual or personality within a particular group. Even though it may appear that the trouble is coming from multiple sources, it is really the leader of the group who is calling the shots and pulling the strings behind the scenes.

It's unfortunate, but one resolute individual that's set on negativity can turn a school into a full-fledge circus. His or her negative energy will quickly spread throughout the school like cancer, dampening the morale of everyone. The only way to appease this individual is to give in to his or her wishes, but doing so is not an option for a principal who is serious about improving the conditions of the school.

Instead of giving in, the principal should work to get rid of the lead troublemaker, and all other troubles will cease. It is not advantageous to negotiate, compromise, or appease a diehard antagonist. Get rid of the person—plain and simple.

There are many educational scholars who write about team building within schools. Many of them suggest that principals try to bring troublemakers into the fold slowly, build their self-esteem, and patiently work with them until they come around and get used to the changes in and around the school.

I've read textbooks that directed principals to give troublemakers a leadership role to recognize their importance and create unity among the staff. The idea behind this philosophy is that since these individuals have some degree of power and influence, they can be used to move reforms forward because they are able to influence other staff members.

I disagree with such a philosophy because most urban schools do not have the luxury of letting the self-serving interest of a few individuals dictate the pace and progress of the school. The principal will have to use a considerable amount of time helping new and underdeveloped employees and those who want to improve and do better for the school.

Urban school principals do not have time to waste on those who are secretly fighting the much-needed changes. Urban schools need reforms that work for students and not those that fit the self-interests of a few staff members with ulterior motives.

Elevating antagonists to leadership roles within the school only feeds into their already-inflated views of their importance. Doing so is likely to hurt more than it would help. Think of all the damage that these individuals have caused and will cause if swift and immediate action isn't taken against them.

I've heard that one rotten apple can spoil an entire basket. Just think of the damage that five, six, or even seven rotten apples can do. If left alone, the troublemakers on the staff will spoil the entire school.

Urban school principals must understand that it is up to them to address issues associated with troublemakers/antagonists toward change. This might be a difficult task for most urban school principals because most of them were trained to use their time for uplifting and encouraging staff members, not to deal with the issues created by a few self-serving individuals. But the reality is that if these individuals are not confronted, then the damage they will do to the school will grow like cancer and be almost impossible to reverse.

The Process

To remove a troublemaker out of the school building, urban school principals must follow a process or a strategic plan of action. This process will not only effectively deal with a troublemaker on the staff but also allow needed reforms to take shape with little resistance. First, principals must identify the leader or dominant figure within a group of troublemakers.

This person may not be the most vocal, but he or she will be the most influential. The other members in the group will revolve around this person like planets do the sun in our solar system. They will mirror the dominant figure's words and ideas—often serving as the mouthpiece for the dominant figure.

It is safe to estimate that an urban school principal can expect to have one lead troublemaker for every 10 employees on the staff. So if the school has a staff of 50, it will have an average of five diehard antagonists. This number could be greater or lesser depending on how the school is grouped (i.e., teams, departments, subjects, or grade levels).

The information presented in chapter 3 involving understanding the school's culture lends itself to helping principals identify who the power players are in the school. If the principal has been in the building for a number of years, she or he should be able to identify who the prime troublemakers are in each area or department of the school.

After identifying the lead troublemaker, principals should move in for a direct attack. By going after the leader or the person whom the mini-troublemakers respect the most, the principal will disrupt the groups focus and central source. Getting rid of the leader will remove the lightening rod that's causing all the sparks of disruption.

The people who follow the lead troublemaker are like leeches. They need something to attach themselves to. In the absence of the lead troublemaker, the school will have a greater chance of unity and cohesion. The leeches will have no choice but to conform to the reforms like everyone else or attach themselves onto the next dominant figure, which should be the principal.

Attacking lead troublemakers involves a two-prong method of separating the leader from his or her support base (the followers) and using progressive discipline to help remove the infectious person from the building. First, let's look at how isolating the troublemaker works in the principal's favor.

The absence of the lead troublemaker from her or his following will loosen one's grip on the group. The only reason why the lead troublemaker acquired supporters in the first place was due to her or his constant presence: the lead troublemaker was always around and able to spread one's cancerous message at the right times when people were vulnerable and able to listen.

I know of a high school principal who had three unrelenting troublemakers on his staff. He used strategic isolation to counteract their divisive actions. First, he structured his staff meetings so that each staff member had a designated seat. The troublemakers were always assigned to seats in the same area, slightly off from the rest of the staff. This prevented the troublemakers from having sidebar conversations with their underlings, and it limited the amount of disruptive outburst during meetings.

After a few meetings, it was obvious to everyone that most of the dissenting voices came from one side of the room and from the same individuals. The principal was able to use the voice and sentiments of the positive majority to silence the troublemakers during staff meetings. After a while, many of the staff members began to stay away from the troublemakers on their own. They didn't want to be around the negativity. The troublemakers' motives became so obvious that they lost most of their power to influence to disrupt.

Next, to further limit their influence, the principal often disrupted the lead troublemakers' interactions with other staff members during the school day. During times when the troublemakers were in collaborative planning meetings with their colleagues (which are prime opportunities for troublemakers to spread their poison), the principal or one of his two assistants would periodically call the troublemakers down to one of their offices or some remote part of the school for banal conversations or menial tasks or to get their opinions on things of little importance—anything to separate them from the group.

Sometimes the troublemakers were asked to come to the office to see one of the administrators, but when they arrived, they were asked to wait. The administrator would have them sit and wait until the collaborative planning period was nearly over.

Another tactic used by this principal was to periodically come into the teachers' lounge during lunch time to use the vending machines when the troublemakers were present, which gave the principal the opportunity to strike polite conversations with other staff and teachers in the lounge. The principal used the time when visiting the lounge to discuss some of the teachers' overall concerns and to further promote the new reforms and vision for the school.

After a while, the type and scope of conversations held by teachers in the lounge were discrete and nonjudgmental of the reforms, because the teachers knew (or believed) that the principal could walk into the lounge at any moment. Unless the troublemakers were prepared to verbally defend their comments openly, they kept silent.

Applying Progressive Discipline

The phase after isolating the lead troublemaker is to apply progressive discipline—the procedures used by administrators when dealing with an employee who violates district rules and policies.

Most urban schools in America are criticized because of poor student performance. The underlying factors associated with any school's poor performance are inefficiency, stagnation, disorganization, and dysfunction on various levels. Within such an environment, there is always someone who either knowingly or unknowingly violates district rules, policies, and procedures.

It is a high probability that if the lead troublemaker is vehemently fighting against much-needed reforms that will improve the school, then he or she has a self-interest that violates one or more of the district's or school's policies. Once the violation has been identified, principals should proceed toward issuing reprimands.

When reprimanding a staff member for violating one of more of the district's rules and policies, principals must adhere to the discipline codes outlined by the school district; or, in cases where a union is involved, principals must follow the disciplinary procedures outlined in the teachers' union contract. Most school employee discipline codes adhere to the following sequence: verbal warning, written warning, written reprimand, second written reprimand, suspension, and termination.

For example, I know of a principal who had an issue with a lead troublemaker in her middle school. The troublemaker was a history teacher and the chairperson for the science department. The principal noticed that the troublemaker had a habit of coming to work 5 to 10 minutes late at least three times per week. Her lateness caused her first-period class to be left out in the hall after the sound of the bell.

Since the history teacher was friends with the security guard on her floor, they had an arrangement where the security guard would open the classroom door to allow the students to go inside until the teacher arrived, which meant that students were left unattended for the time that the teacher wasn't present in the classroom.

The principal also observed the troublemaker leaving campus for lunch on a regular basis. Teachers leaving campus for lunch didn't violate any district policy, but the troublemaker would often return 5 to 10 minutes late for the start of her fourth period—a direct violation of school policy. Again, the security guard on the floor would open the classroom door in an effort to get the students out of the hallway, but again the students were left unattended until the teacher arrived just like with the first period class.

After observing this pattern for two consecutive days, the principal gave the teacher a verbal warning. The behavior repeated a few days later, so the principal issued a written warning. Two weeks after receiving the written warning, the teacher was late to her fourth-period class, but the security guard did not let the students into the classroom. The guard was engaged in a situation in the cafeteria, so he couldn't let the students in. The students were out in the hall well after the bell sounded.

A fight broke out in front of the teacher's classroom. Students from neighboring classrooms ran out into the hall to see the commotion (some students who were coming from lunch participated in the fight as well), which added to the severity of the situation. After the dust settled and the students were disciplined, the teacher was suspended for willful neglect of duty.

Once the troublemaker came back from her suspension, she had no influence over the staff members who once followed her. The suspension was a powerful form of isolation. The troublemaker was not able to cause any trouble while she was out, and her absence sent a stern message to the rest of her group. They learned that employees who violate school rules and policies will suffer consequences no matter who they are.

When dealing with troublemakers on the staff, urban school principals also need to be aware that some troublemakers may not violate any of the rules or policies. If that is the case, then principals should attack the troublemaker's followers to lessen the damage that lead troublemakers cause. It is safe to say that one or more of the troublemaker's group members are chronic violators of some school policy or are lacking in some form of their job responsibilities.

Attacking the followers weakens the lead troublemaker's base of support and loosens their power hold. Without the support and allegiance of the followers, lead troublemakers stand alone and will be ineffective at causing dissention and negating needed reforms. Dealing with troublemakers sends a powerful message throughout the school of what will and will not be tolerated.

It also increases the principal's authority because lead troublemakers are generally the ones who hold an ample amount of power and influence in the school. Their authority can be even greater than that of the principal if she or he is new to the building or lacks the knowledge to deal with them. Disciplining these individuals automatically elevates the principal into a higher status within the hearts and minds of the other school employees on the staff.

Disciplining lead troublemakers also gives hope to the employees who are in agreement with the reforms. They will step up, become leaders themselves, and take action that will help change the culture of the school into a positive one.

There are two main reasons why troublemakers exist and become effective within urban schools. The first is that there are too many fearful urban school principals. They are afraid to deal with any form of conflict; they are afraid of the least bit of friction; they are afraid of making someone upset; or they are afraid to have any unfavorable news reach central office.

Many principals fear having a grievance filed against them. They are afraid of having people complain about them, which could cause them to lose their positions. To avoid making anyone upset, they try to keep everyone happy, usually at the expense of the school's overall success.

Too many urban school principals are overly concerned about trying to please everyone with whom they come into contact. The truth is that it's impossible for school leaders to make everyone happy all the time—especially in a school with a history of failure and in need of changes. Some individuals do not have the school's best interest at heart, so why would a principal want to make those people happy?

When any kind of real systemic changes occur, it's inevitable that some people are going to be disgruntled. Urban school principals must accept this and know that they can't always be people pleasers. If the much-needed reforms displease a small group of dissenters, then so be it. The objective is to improve the school, not please a few individuals who don't have the school's overall best interest at heart.

The second and just as prevalent reason why troublemakers thrive in urban schools is that many urban school principals don't organize their time wisely. Time management is one of the most sacred and important assets of any school principal.

Many principals are too bogged down dealing with problems associated with student discipline, irate parents, obligations from central office, budget and resource limitations, maintenance issues, and a host of other problems. They don't perceive they have the time to effectively deal with troublemakers on the staff, so they prioritize and put these types of employees further down their "to do" lists.

Also, some school districts have ironclad union contracts that make it almost impossible to remove an ineffective employee. Due to the varied responsibilities of the principal, combined with the difficulty of removing an ineffective employee, some principals elect to leave troublesome staff members alone instead of devoting time toward removing them completely from the school building. But what these principals don't realize is that unless the troublemakers on the staff are totally removed, the other problems within the school will remain (dissention, low morale, disunity, inappropriate behavior, low output, inefficiency, disorganization, etc.).

Furthermore, when dealing with troublemakers, principals must document everything—every conversation, e-mail, conference, letter, memo, and action associated with the employee's infractions. The documentation should contain the date, time, and all issues discussed between the principal and the employee in question. Principals should also document any interventions or strategies shared with the employee for improvement.

Extensive documentation is good because before any aggressive action is taken against a school employee, such as suspension or termination, someone (e.g., hearing officer, union representative, or central office administrator) will want to know about the types of actions the principal has taken leading up to the disciplinary action.

If there isn't any sufficient documentation or efforts to correct the matter on the principal's behalf, then it's unlikely that the employee in question will be suspended, terminated, or removed from the school. The troublemaker will not only return to the school in his or her former position but also have a renewed spirit—having won a victory over the principal.

This is dangerous because such a victory will elevate the troublemaker's status among the other employees, making him or her even harder to deal with in the future. Principals should play it safe and document everything. Also, without proper documentation and adherence to the steps outlined for progressive discipline, more attention will be placed on the lack of documentation instead of where the emphasis should be—on the employee's deficiencies.

Removing a problem employee from the school is very time-consuming, but the work must be done; it should be one of the principal's top priorities. Unless troublemakers commit some gross infraction, like having inappropriate contact with a student or coming to work intoxicated, a safe estimation for the amount of time it will take to remove the average troublemaker from the school building is one school year.

Final note: If an employee disagrees with the principal, has an outspoken personality, or questions one or more of the principal's actions or reform initiatives doesn't make her or him a troublemaker. Having dialogue among staff and expressing various opinions and points of view are healthy components for any school's growth and progress. Principals should not only accept various opinions but encourage such behavior from the school's staff.

Too often, leaders think they can change the negative attitudes and opinions of individuals by merely writing policies or issuing reprimands, but those things are just one aspect of creating effective change. The real work behind changing negative attitudes lies with changing the culture of the school.

The environment has to be a place where people feel connected, valued, and appreciated. They must believe that the work they're contributing really matters and is a significant part of the school's overall success. School employees have to believe that they're making a difference and that things can and will get better.

The principal must spearhead a culture where the most important thing is whether students are achieving. The second-most important thing is making all staff members feel valued and appreciated. If all staff members are focused on their individual responsibilities as they relate to students and if they feel good about what they're doing, then the troublemakers will be irrelevant.

When a school has a negative school culture, troublemakers have room to maneuver, stir anxieties, and cause dissention among their colleagues. But in a positive school culture, troublemakers will not be able to use their time, energy, and influence in divisive ways, because there will be too many positive influences to combat their negative efforts. Therefore, the school's climate will become self-regulating. The principal will not have to do anything, because the people around the troublemakers will take care of them—putting an end to dissention and giving reform initiatives a chance to blossom.

SEVEN

Stagnation and Inefficiency

Most human beings become stagnate and comfortable with their thinking and environmental conditions in the absence of a strong force pressing the need for change. When a certain level of comfort is achieved, some humans lose their work ethic, intrinsic motivation, and ability to think of new and innovative ideas. Unfortunately for urban schools, many stakeholders (teachers, parents, community leaders, administrators, etc.) suffer from stagnation.

They have become comfortable with the chaos, low performance, inefficiency, and dysfunction surrounding them. They've become too accepting of the way that things are rather than looking toward the possibilities of the future. Many have given up hope and stopped believing that things can be better.

After stagnation has set in, the next step in the downward spiral is inefficiency. Inefficient schools have employees who don't pay attention to details, who neglect their job tasks and responsibilities, and who are careless with their actions and attitudes; they don't move with any sense of urgency, nor do they take their jobs seriously. They take their time when doing the simplest of tasks, and they rarely give their best effort. Over periods of time, inefficiency becomes a permanent way of doing business within the school and a common mind-set of the school's staff.

This mentality is reinforced because they've witnessed previous changes in leadership and other halfhearted attempts at reform go by, and the school remains the same. The people who are affected most by inefficient practices are the ones whom the school is supposed to serve (parents, students, and the greater community). When the school is not organized and operating in an efficient manner, these stakeholders become quickly frustrated and lose faith in the school's ability to provide a quality education.

For example, I know of a situation involving a high school principal with a student population of 1,600. The principal, in his second year, wanted to make sure that students' schedules were processed over the summer and sent out via postal mail two weeks before the first day of school. In his first year, the process was handled terribly, so the principal didn't want repeat the scenario.

To ensure the work would be done, the principal arranged for two of his three counselors to be on paid duty over the summer. At the end of each week, the principal asked the counselors for an update. Each time, the counselors told him that things were progressing according to schedule. They ensured that the students' schedules would be ready and mailed as planned.

On the day the schedules were supposed to be mailed, the principal discovered that the counselors were far behind: only a third of the schedules were ready for mailing. Since the schedules were not ready as planned, the principal decided to have the staff finish the schedules so that they can be ready for students on the first day of school. He told them to put the schedules in alphabetical order according to the students' last names and to divide the schedules among the three counselors for distribution.

He also told them to set up three tables in the cafeteria so that when students arrived in the morning on the first day, they could go to the appropriate table and receive their schedules before moving to their first-period class. He concluded by telling the counselors they had to be ready to distribute schedules by 7:45 am because students would be allowed to enter the building by 8 am. The three counselors agreed to the principal's alternative plan and promised to be ready.

On the first day of school, the counselors still didn't have all the schedules ready for distribution. To make matters worse, they were not set up and ready by the designated time of 7:45 am. The earliest counselor arrived at her table by 8:25 am, another came in at 8:30 am, and the last one came at 9:00 am.

The third counselor didn't work over the summer, but the principal also instructed her and told her the designated time to set up. Due to the counselors' inefficiency and failure to be in position, the students quickly became disgruntled and frustrated.

Many students had parents or relatives accompanying them the first day. The adults also became upset at the inefficiency and unpreparedness of the counselors. Several angry parents stormed the main office demanding to see the principal. One parent became so upset that she got into a shouting match with one of the office aides at the front desk. The scene became so disruptive that the school's security team had to remove the irate parent from the school building.

Some students used the situation as an excuse to roam the halls and cause trouble. Once large groups of students started to loiter in the halls;

most of the teachers closed their classroom doors to isolate themselves for the chaos. Many teachers sat in empty classrooms for most the day while the school's administrators and security tried to clear students out of the halls and get things under control.

Around lunchtime, one of the students roaming the halls pulled the fire alarm. Everyone had to evacuate the building. To make matters worse, one angry parent contacted the local media, so reporters were on school grounds while students were being evacuated from the school building due to the false fire.

THE HARD TRUTH

Unfortunately, this scenario and similar situations are not uncommon in many urban schools across America. There are very few isolated events that happen within a school setting. Most that occur are cyclical and will affect other areas, whether directly or indirectly.

It goes without saying that the counselors' behavior in this scenario was unprofessional and unacceptable, but they shouldn't be attributed all the blame. The principal should share some of the responsibility for the chaotic first day as well. He allowed the counselors' actions to perpetuate because he didn't properly hold them accountable.

The counselors were not appropriately monitored, so they took advantage. Their neglect of duty not only had an impact on the school's overall efficiency and functioning but also adversely affected the customer service in the front office, the school's safety and security, and the quality of instruction delivered that day.

If a school's environment and staff climate are lackadaisical and employees are allowed to operate without any sense of urgency, then that's how the employees will respond. If there isn't a fair and appropriate amount of accountability, which should be built within the school's culture, then scenarios like the aforementioned one will continue to exist within urban schools.

Urban school principals should set the tone for their schools and work to maintain a cultural climate that fosters behaviors that will combat the negative effects of stagnation and inefficiency.

Disrupt Their Routines

There are methods for dealing with school employees who suffer from stagnation and inefficiency. The best way to handle any employee who is stagnant is to break up his or her routine. Do not allow such staff to become comfortable with a familiar pattern or action for a prolonged period. Constantly give them challenges, new tasks, and varied responsibilities.

If they are accustomed to sitting down in the office while performing their duties, then give them duties that will cause them to stand, or give them tasks that will periodically take them out of the office. Breaking up their familiar patterns will light a spark in them and reduce the stagnation that comes with performing the same routines and duties, or it will become incredibly obvious to the principal that they don't have what it takes to maintain their positions of employment.

When varying an employee's routines, principals have to make sure the new tasks and challenges are applicable to the employee's title or position. For example, a teacher should not be assigned tasks associated with a custodian or secretary, but a teacher could be asked to perform additional tasks, such as chair a school-based committee, develop a yearbook, create a school newsletter, update the school's website, or spearhead an after-school program or club for students. Principals could also change a teacher's classroom location or the subject that he or she will teach from one year to the next. They could even change the subject that the teacher will teach for a given year (as long as the teacher is qualified).

Along with disrupting normal routines, the principal can try to incorporate a system of rewards or spark friendly competition among the staff. Rewards and competition can serve as the catalyst that some employees need in order to lift them out of a slump and get their minds and bodies motivated and focused.

Give Deadlines for Completing Tasks

The second phase in the process involves giving employees deadlines for completing tasks. Whenever a task or request is given, the principal should specify a date or time for completion. Giving a deadline will place the right amount of pressure, or "heat," on the employees. They'll understand that they must produce because the principal is not only monitoring but also expecting results within a particular time frame.

Far too often, urban school principals fail to hold every individual on the school's staff accountable. If the principal doesn't give specific tasks or deadlines for employees to meet, some will do nothing or the bare minimum, which is how schools become nonproductive institutions. The overarching goal is to create a work environment where employees know they must come to perform.

Varying tasks, challenges, and deadlines for the completion of tasks will be enough for most school employees to shake the bands of stagnation. But there will always be a select few who will not change no matter what. They will not rise to the occasion, nor will they meet any deadline given to them.

They will be either too lazy, incompetent, or too stubborn to change their ways or try a different way of doing things. They will put up resistance and have excuses for their inadequacies and shortcomings. When faced with such obdurateness, the only option for principals is to proceed with progressive discipline. There has to be consequences for every negligent action.

I speak about the use of progressive discipline in chapter 6. The reprimands delivered to the employee will increase the pressure on them to perform, because if they don't change the negative behavior, they will be out of a job eventually. The threat of losing one's job is enough to shake most people up. If the possibility of losing employment isn't enough to change their behavior, then they don't deserve a position within the school building. The principal should work to have them removed as soon as possible.

Final note: the overall tone of the school's environment and the temperament of the employees start with the school's leader. He or she must lead by example. If the principal has a lackadaisical attitude, lacks purpose and a sense of urgency, or is comfortable with mediocrity and failure, then the rest of the school's staff will display the same behaviors. Likewise, if the principal moves with a sense of purpose and conviction, then the employees will usually respond accordingly.

It is also important to note that not all aspects of inefficiency and stagnation merit a reprimand. Oftentimes, principals merely need to model the correct way to perform the tasks, or they need to provide examples and support. This will give employees more confidence and renew their spirits brighter than issuing a reprimand or disciplinary action.

The business of education is a serious one, especially when dealing with students who in many cases come from economically, socially, and psychologically oppressed situations. All school employees should feel a certain level of pressure that comes along with performing well and having the desire to do a good job. There is no time for complacency and inefficiency. Urban school principals must serve as the pressing force that ignites change and the primary source for getting all school employees moving in the right direction.

EIGHT

Disruptive Students

Most urban schools with a history of failure have bad reputations that precede them. They could have some really great programs and employees, but they are overshadowed by certain events that shaped the school's reputation. Many factors contribute to such egregious reputations, but one issue leading the pack is the schools' inability to deal with disruptive student behaviors.

In urban schools, disruptive students are more talked about than low test scores, low achievement, or any other aspect of school performance. It is also the issue that causes urban school teachers the most anxiety and nervousness. Disruptive students not only hinder a teacher's ability to teach effectively but they can also make teachers question the value of their work and lower their self-efficacy.

The negative attention associated with disruptive students also plays a major role in the school's ability to attract and maintain qualified teachers, as well as establish and maintain the confidence of parents. The bad reputations of many urban schools have prompted many highly qualified teachers to seek employment in nonurban districts and caused many parents to vote against levies and seek alternative options for their children (vouchers, homeschooling, etc.). This translates into low student enrollment, poor achievement, budget cuts, and layoffs.

Disruptive students are difficult for school officials for various reasons. Not only do they hinder the instructional process, but they also exhibit a host of other behaviors that adversely affect the school's cultural climate: they try to intimidate, bully, disrespect authority, and fail to follow the simplest rules and requests from adults.

Most people in the educational community often attribute disruptive student behavior to a lack of parenting and home training, but that may not be true for the majority of students who attend urban school. Many disruptive behaviors that students display are a direct result of the students' environmental community conditions. Educators make a huge mistake when they eliminate the effects that poverty or low socioeconomic living conditions have on a school's ability to properly educate its students.

Certain behaviors, usually essential for urban students' survival, are culturally imbedded into urban communities. Despite their necessity, many of the behaviors are not aligned with being successful in school.

For example, most low socioeconomic urban communities lack the necessary resources needed to flourish and remain viable. The lack of resources (jobs, money, health care, food, transportation, housing, safety and security, etc.) creates an emptiness that's deeply embedded throughout these communities. The void that exists within low socioeconomic communities perpetuates a "crabs in the barrel" syndrome among residents, which is perpetuated within the fabric of the community's culture until it becomes a natural way of living and thinking.

This is one reason why some kids living in poor urban communities are able to commit senseless crimes and acts of violence over things like a pair of gym shoes, a coat, or some other "worthless" material item. Urban residents most affected by this mentality will do anything to acquire what they deem essential for their survival, no matter how menial the item or who they have to hurt to get it.

Let's look at another close example to see how the effects of community poverty have on students' behavior in school. I once had a student who had four grown siblings living at home with their mother in a cramped two-bedroom apartment in the projects. The student's sister, who was 22 years old, had a newborn baby living in the apartment as well.

When the mother cooked a meal during any part of the day (breakfast, lunch, or dinner), it was rarely enough food for everyone to get a sufficient portion, and if one of the family members was not present when the food was served, then chances were that the absent family member probably wouldn't eat that particular meal.

It wasn't unusual for family members in the household to argue and fight over food. Drinking someone's soda left in the refrigerator or eating someone's piece of chicken could easily turn into all out warfare. Similar arguments also took place over clothes and the television.

Since there were only two bedrooms, sleeping arrangements were a perpetual issue. The student's mother, sister, and young baby slept in one room together, while the other members had to sleep in the other bedroom or on the living room couch. The sleeping arrangements were set on an unspoken rule of first come, first serve.

The prime spaces to occupy were the single twin bed in the second bedroom, the living room couch, and the space on the living room floor next to the television. Just as with food, there were often many arguments and fights among family members over who claimed what sleeping area first.

Some might ask, what does this scenario have to do with disruptive students and discipline in urban schools? The scenario is an example, or backdrop, of why some urban students are disruptive in school, which leads to a school's overall discipline problem.

Schools generally try to foster supportive environments of collaboration, teamwork, and sharing. Most schools also try to stress the importance of students being polite, acting cooperatively, and putting the group's needs over individual ones. With regard to issues of conflict, students are asked to seek adult assistance, resolve conflicts peacefully, use words to settle disputes, and avoid violence.

These kinds of ideals do not completely mesh with the home environment of many urban students. For many urban students, aggression and violence are a way of life. The inability to assert oneself aggressively could literally mean being deprived of a basic fundamental need (food, clothing, shelter, safety, etc.). The following excerpt, from Ruby Payne's book *A Framework for Understanding Poverty* (2005), explains it perfectly:

> Being able to physically fight or have someone fight for you is important to survive in poverty. Yet, in middle class, being able to negotiate conflict is crucial. Many times the fists are used in poverty because the words are neither available nor respected.

In the aforementioned scenario, the student's home life sets the conditions to behave and act in one way at home, but those same behaviors eventually gets the student into trouble at school. Something as simple as someone sitting in another student's assigned seat, an accidental bumping that causes a student to drop his or her lunch onto the floor, one student taking another student's pencil, or a simple verbal disagreement among students can easily turn into a full-blown crisis for a teacher or administrator to handle.

Since most adults working in urban schools do not live in poverty, nor were they typically raised in communities similar to those where urban students live, many of the behaviors urban students display are misinterpreted and misunderstood by most adults whom they interact with while in the school setting. Most adults in the school building will be clueless about why their students are so volatile and unmanageable.

The scenario is not uncommon; in fact, some of the actual circumstances of many urban students are a lot worse. It is not a far stretch to take the same scenario and change or add different components. For example, the same housing conditions could exist with the older siblings selling drugs, carrying illegal guns, or sexually abusing the younger siblings; the older sister could have multiple children instead of one or have a boyfriend also living in the cramped apartment; the mother could be addicted to drugs or alcohol or neglectful in her duties as a parent. These dynamics are a real part of the lives of many students who attend urban schools, which undoubtedly have an effect on teaching and learning, classroom management, and student discipline.

If an entire school is filled with students of similar or worse environmental community backgrounds, the school will eventually assume the same cultural characteristics. Not all students who live in poverty have such extreme home living situations, but if the dominant culture mirrors what I described, the less-affected students will follow suit by shaping their behavior to meet the conditions of the school's dominate culture, which will be necessary for their survival and acceptance while in school. For example, if a relatively good student is surrounded by peers who are frequently disrespectful to adults, cutting classes, or not taking learning seriously, then the seemingly good student will take on those characteristics to blend in and gain acceptance. Urban school principals must not only effectively deal with disruptive students but also create a school environment that counteracts most of the detrimental conditions associated with poverty and urban/inner-city living.

THE HARD TRUTH

As I mentioned previously, many components of this book are interconnected. The tenets mentioned in chapters 1, 2, 4, 5, and 10 lend toward helping principals effectively deal with disruptive students. Urban school principals have to use the knowledge gained from such areas and apply it toward creating a system for how the school will collectively handle student disciplinary issues.

I often compare students to the natural element known as water. Water is a very important element used to necessitate life on Earth for all living creatures. It's a fluid substance that takes the shape of the container it's in. Water can be soft and gentle like a flowing stream, or it can be violent like a hurricane. Water has the ability to deteriorate any solid substance over a prolonged period.

Students are similar to water because they are the lifeblood of schools. All the work that educators do, as well as the existence of the profession, relies on having students. Student enrollment is the engine that drives all schools. It affects every aspect of operations—from funding and hiring staff to the types of programs and courses offered. Without the students, there is no school.

Similar to water, students shape their behavior and adapt to fit whatever conditions or environment they're in. If the school's environment is loose, unstructured, unorganized, and dysfunctional, then most of the students will behave accordingly. But if the environment is the opposite—structured, organized, and conducive to learning—then students will shape their behavior to fit such a paradigm. Urban school principals must create a safe and orderly academic environment for all students.

To deal with disruptive students and counteract some of the negative forces from their environmental conditions, urban school principals should employ a two-pronged tactical approach. The first tactic involves short-term, immediate action on the principal's part, while the other is more long-term and systemic. When the strategies are employed together, disruptive students will have minimum opportunities to cause problems within the school.

The Process

The manner in which the school handles disruptive students starts and ends with the principal. He or she will set the tone for the rest of the employees and students alike. Therefore, at the start of the school year, the principal should declare his or her stance on student discipline. One's discipline philosophy should be espoused to parents, faculty and staff, and students (individually and schoolwide).

It should be communicated in multiple ways as well (newsletters, websites, handbooks, banners and wall postings, etc.). After the principal has verbally communicated his or her expectations for student behavior, many of the stakeholders are going to test the principal to see if he or she is really serious. People will want to see if the words are going to be followed with effective action.

Dealing with disruptive students is similar to dealing with troublemakers on the staff. It's a simple process of finding the ringleader and attacking. As stated previously, when trouble occurs, it usually can be traced to a single individual—the dominant personality of a particular group. This person is somehow able to captivate followers and win over the affection, respect, and loyalty of their admirers.

Most school-age students, regardless of their grade level, are trying to blend in and be accepted by their peers. They value individuality, but at the same time, there is a strong desire for peer acceptance. They don't want to stand out too much for fear of being ostracized from the majority group.

If the school's culture is one in which disruptive students can operate with impunity, then the rest of the students will assimilate to the negative school culture and imitate the disruptive characteristics displayed by everyone else in their peer group. As time passes, the dysfunction caused by disruptive students will be accepted by everyone as the norm. Students will misinterpret the dysfunction as the proper way to behave while in school because that's what everyone else is doing.

The principal must find the source of the disruption and stop it immediately. It is very easy to find the sources of the student disruption, but to do so, the principal must be visible and mobile. She or he must be out and about in the places where students are—the halls, restrooms, cafeteria, and the classrooms, to name a few.

Principals can't afford to be confined to the office or spend the majority of their time stuck in meetings. Being visible and mobile is how urban school principals can get an accurate assessment of how students are behaving within the school. In a short period, faces will become familiar, and the patterns of student behaviors will become apparent.

Being visible in places where students are will also give the principal insight to which students are the most disruptive. These students will stand out because of two main reasons. First, they exhibit behavior a little more pretentious than normal, which becomes progressively worse within a short period.

Second, disruptive students always have people following them. The followers usually look at the ringleader as a source of amusement; they want to see what he or she is going to do next. The ringleader continues to act up to maintain the followers' attention, creating a cyclical relationship: the more attention the ringleader gets, the more he or she will act out; the more the ringleader continues to act out, the more followers he or she will attract.

For example, I know a former principal who once walked into the cafeteria during lunchtime and saw a male student standing on a lunchroom table with four to five other students cheering him on. The student was pretending that he was on a stage performing in front of an audience. The principal saw the student's behavior, turned around, and walked in the opposite direction away from the scene in the cafeteria.

A month later, the same student was yelling at the top of his lungs at a female student (the young woman was supposedly his girlfriend). The male student used various profane words and made several threatening gestures with his hands while two of his friends laughed in the background. The situation caused such a disturbance that several students and teachers came out of their classrooms to see what was going on in the hallway. The principal also heard the student's tirade in the hall, but instead of addressing it while it was happening, the principal walked in the opposite direction again—pretending not to have heard or seen the incident.

About two weeks after that, the same male student came into the school building with a 24-inch snake around his next. No one knows exactly how he was able to smuggle the snake into the building pass the security guards, but he caused a huge stir to say the least. As the bell sounded to signal the passing of classes, the disruptive student paraded up and down the second floor hallway with several of his friends.

Many of the female students began to scream and run, while most of the male students laughed and cheered. The principal heard the commotion, saw the student with the huge snake around his neck, but behaved as he did previously by neglecting to address the student. He walked away from the incident.

This example may sound like something made for a television series, but it actually happened. I'm not saying that all disruptive students will display the same behaviors as the ones in this example, but as principals become more visible within their schools, student misbehaviors will be immediately noticeable. If the misbehaviors go unchecked, they will become progressively worse over time. The worst part is that other students will witness the disruptions and the administration's lack of corrective action, which will eventually trigger negative behaviors from them as well.

Dealing with disruptive students is courageous work because many principals will often make a conscious effort to try to avoid confrontation of any kind (students, staff, parents, etc.). They do this because they don't want to feel the backlash from students and/or their parents. Urban school principals who are afraid to confront disruptive students are indirectly sending the message that the adverse student behaviors being displayed in school are okay.

What's even more damaging is that the other students who are watching will see the principal's lack of action as a reason to display similar disruptive behavior. There were some students who saw the incident in my example with the snake as a positive one because not only did the disruptive student get a lot of attention from his peers, but he seemingly got away with causing a disturbance. Some students will view this as a good way to gain attention and acceptance from their peers.

The principal should immediately confront disruptive students as soon as they manifest themselves. When misbehavior is immediately confronted, the principal solidifies his or her authority among students—creating an aura of respect. He or she also sends the message to the other students who are watching that such disruptions to the school's environment are not tolerated.

The followers will look at the situation and dare not commit the same infraction. If the principal is unclear about whom the ringleaders are, then he or she should select the first student seen violating a rule and make an example out of him or her. For example, I once worked in a high school that had a policy prohibiting students from using cell phones during school hours. According to the district's student code of conduct, cell phones were to be confiscated and returned after a parent conference on the first offense—followed by 3 days of out-of-school suspension for the second offense, with another parent conference upon the student's return.

The consequences became progressively worse, with 5, 7, and 10 days of out-of-school suspension for the third, fourth, and fifth offenses, respectively (each followed by a parent conference). For the sixth violation, students were to be recommended for expulsion. If a student refused to release his or her cell phone to any school official at any time when seen violating the rule, the student would be automatically suspended for failure to follow a reasonable request (regardless of where one stood within the level of consequences).

At the beginning of the school year, I had a schoolwide assembly where I addressed many student discipline codes and policies. I emphasized the cell phone policy after finding out that students blatantly violated this rule in the past. After the assembly, I decided that I was going to confiscate the cell phone of every student violating the rule, since they were previously warned.

Immediately after the assembly, I saw a female student having an intense conversation on her cell phone while in the hallway. I politely interrupted the student and asked for the phone. When she refused, I called for security and had her escorted to the office and prepared for suspension. A few minutes later, I saw another student talking on his cell phone.

I asked him for his phone and recited the cell phone policy for students, but he also refused to give me the phone, although he did give me a few choice words in the process. As with the first situation, I called security and had this student escorted to the office and prepared for suspension. By the time students were cleared out of the hall, I had 10 students of various grades in my office for violating the cell phone policy. Each one of their parents were contacted, and each one received three days of out-of-school suspension.

I repeated the same actions everyday over a 10-day period. Each day, fewer students were being suspended. By the start of the 11th day, students were not using their cell phones during school hours (at least not in plain sight)—and it continued that way throughout the school year. Students got the message that such behavior was not going to be tolerated. My aggressive and persistent actions spread throughout the school like wildfire. The onlookers saw how the violators were dealt with, and they did not want to experience the same fate. Teachers and other staff members also became comfortable with enforcing the policy because they knew that I would back them up.

There were some students who were caught violating the rule and gave up their phones without hesitation. They knew that the consequences were being enforced, so they made the wise decision to give up their phones and have their parents come to the school to retrieve them during a conference instead of being suspended from school. Another aspect that contributed to the students' speedy compliance was the actions of the parents.

The parents quickly became tired of having to come to the school to conference over the same issue, so they helped to enforce the school's policy by making their children comply. Many parents threatened to take away their child's privilege of having a cell phone if the child didn't comply with the school's rules and policies.

The same method can be applied to other situations because all student misbehaviors are addressed in the school district's behavioral code of conduct for students. Principals can't be afraid to address disruptive students when they immediately display negative behaviors. There will be some students who will not comply and some parents who will not be supportive. Also, there will be students who will respond disrespectfully when confronted and some parents who will do the same when contacted.

Some parents do not hold their children accountable and would rather try to make the school or the principal out to be the villain instead of correcting their child's conduct. These types of parents will even try to go above the principal's head and contact central office to complain. This happened to me regarding the cell phone scenario.

A small number of parents complained about me and my actions, but my superiors supported me despite each complaint. I was able to continue operating in the same manner because I followed the code of conduct to the letter. The school district had to either support what I was doing or change the entire policy for that particular item. I wasn't concerned about any backlash from parents or anyone else, because I was operating within the guidelines set by the district. Knowing that I was operating within the district's guidelines gave me the courage and confidence to continue.

Create a Schoolwide Discipline Plan

Last but definitely not least, urban school principals must create a schoolwide discipline plan that emphasizes rewards for good behavior instead of punishment for bad behavior. It's not enough to target the disruptive students when you see them—that's merely one aspect of it. To sustain long-term positive student behavior, it must be part of the overall school culture.

The schoolwide behavior plan must be a global plan, one adopted and implemented by everyone on the school's staff that interacts with students. Its creation should involve as many stakeholders as possible to ensure that student behavioral expectations are shared, understood, and perpetuated by all.

Many students misbehave simply because they don't feel any genuine connection to the school or anyone working within it. There are many students in urban schools who don't feel valued or welcomed while in school. A student's disconnection from school, coupled with some deficiencies associated with her or his home and environmental living conditions, provides the perfect mix for a disruptive student environment.

A behavior plan that's incentive based will not only foster a positive response from students but also assist with helping school officials establish rapport and create deeper relationships with students that will curtail most adverse student behavioral problems. Rewarding students for positive behavior also signals to students which behaviors are acceptable in the school setting. It also creates an overall positive school culture, which causes students to adapt their behavior to meet the expectations set.

Every school is different; each has its own culture and ways of doing things. Due to the nuances and complexities of most urban schools and the various student behavioral issues faced, the schoolwide incentive-based behavioral plan must be specific to each setting. There is no "one size fits all" or "cookie-cutter" approach to developing and implementing such a plan in an urban school.

According to Colvin (2007), developing an effective schoolwide discipline plan should involve the following:

- Determining the school's needs as they relate to student discipline
- Establishing a building leadership team
- Setting schoolwide behavioral expectations
- Allocating time for teaching and modeling the behavioral expectations
- Maintaining the behavioral expectations by correcting problem behaviors

Establishing an incentive-based schoolwide discipline plan is important not only for a school's cultural climate but also for reducing interruptions in teaching. It also makes students feel safe, increases student achievement, and prevents many problem situations and behaviors before they occur.

NINE
Academic Instruction

One of the main reasons why student achievement is low in many urban schools is that there is a lack of sound instructional design, implementation, and delivery on behalf of teachers. Some teachers working in urban schools rely too heavily on lecturing, direct instruction, textbook assignments ("Read the chapter and answer the questions"), copying, videos, and note taking. Within a short period, their lessons become stale, uninteresting, boring, and unsuited for improving student achievement.

It's unfortunate, but many urban school teachers are in survival mode. They're just trying to make it through the day without any major incidents. They're more concerned with ways to keep students "busy," instead of engaging students with meaningful assignments that are appropriately challenging and rigorous. They use the same, recycled lesson plans year after year without making any improvements or adjustments.

These kinds of teachers are not in tune with the students' academic needs and deficiencies from one year to the next, so the methods they use for instructional delivery do not connect with them. They may know and understand the content they're teaching, but it's not being delivered in ways that are edifying to students. Therefore, the quality of instruction that students receive is minimal at best.

Ineffective classroom instruction can adversely affect other areas of the school's culture (classroom management, truancy, graduation rates, students' attention span and behavior, and suspension and expulsion rates, to name a few). I'm not putting all the problems of urban schools on the shoulders of teachers, because they're not solely responsible. Fingers can be pointed at many people and at various factors. But one thing I know for sure is that urban school principals have to carry some of them blame as well.

I believe that the issues affecting some urban school teachers (low morale, low self-efficacy, inadequate instructional design and delivery, lack of support, etc.) is a direct result of the schools' overall inefficiency, lack of leadership, and disorganization, which falls directly on the head of principals. In most cases, when school leaders are deficient or negligent in their basic job functions, everyone working within the school is adversely affected—especially teachers and the quality of instruction they're able to render to students.

Some of the teachers who are in survival mode are in this condition because they never received support, direction, guidance, or counsel from their principals. Due to the absence of good leadership, many teachers quickly go into survival mode. Instead of developing their practice, they start developing characteristics not beneficial for themselves as professionals or for their students as learners.

In this state, they often latch on to the nearest dominant figure that seemingly shares their frustrations and shows them the best way to survive in the current dysfunctional school climate. In most cases, the dominant figure who gains their trust will typically be one of the lead troublemakers discussed in chapter 6. Before you know it, the teacher who was struggling to survive will easily be turned into a member of the lead troublemaker's group.

Ineffective leaders breed ineffective teachers; ineffective teachers breed low-performing students; low-performing students breed low academic achievement; and low academic achievement equates to a failing school. Urban school teachers work with students who present some of the most challenging issues any teaching professionals will face. Therefore, they need support from administrators that will assist them with instructional methods and interventions suited for the needs of the students being served. Anything short of this is an injustice to not only the students but also the teachers and their growth and development.

THE HARD TRUTH

Any solid academic program for students relies on two vital components. If urban school principals can implement them, student achievement will improve instantly. The two components are (1) to hire the right teachers and (2) to provide all teachers with sufficient support. An organization is only as good as the employees working within it. Urban schools need effective teachers who are committed to providing a quality education for all students, regardless of the challenges they present.

Hire the Right Teachers

Hiring the right teachers is probably one of the most important tasks that urban school principals will perform to improve the overall quality of instruction delivered to students. Due to the complexities of most urban schools and the issues generally associated with them, it takes a special kind of teacher to work in an urban school and be effective. Contrary to what one might think, the right teacher is not necessarily the one with the extensive resume, the higher-level degree, the abundant years of experience, or the recognition as "highly qualified" by some governing body.

Although these characteristics are desirable, they don't necessarily translate into an effective teacher who has to work with students with diverse and assorted needs and backgrounds. Principals shouldn't use the aforementioned teacher qualities as the primary factors for filling vacant teaching positions within urban schools. When making hiring decisions, urban school principals should place more value on a teacher's passion and commitment to the profession of teaching. The extent of a person's resume should come second.

There are many educators who are working in urban schools for all the wrong reasons. Although they may be credentialed, their motivation for working with urban students is not altruistic. Some are there because they're participating in government programs that will repay their college student loans for the time they're working in distressed/impoverished schools. Others work in urban schools because they're trying to gain experience until a more desirable position becomes available in an affluent district. In other cases, some teachers working in urban schools couldn't get a job anywhere else; the urban school districts were the only ones that would hire them.

These types might hold a degree, be highly qualified, and know the content of their subject areas, but they are the wrong types for urban students. These kinds of teachers will not have the intestinal fortitude to deal with the issues and circumstances they'll face in the classroom. They will lack the desire to go the extra mile needed for the success of the students they've been commissioned to teach.

Urban schools need teachers who are passionate and committed. These kinds of teachers will not fold under pressure. Their desire to help students will serve as their motivation to push forward when faced with challenges from students, parents, administrators, and the community. They will be willing to go an extra mile to reach students, even when they are resisting. The right teachers will also take time to establish rapport and make genuine connections with students and their families, which is the foundation for improving student achievement and academic performance.

The positive connections that teachers are able to establish and maintain with urban students will serve as the basis for improving all aspects of the classroom—instructional delivery, classroom management, student participation, student behavior, grades and academic performance, and so on. When teachers consistently display a genuine interest in students and work to build rapport, students will generally respond by giving their best effort.

Positive rapport with students leads to the teacher gaining the students' trust. When students trust teachers, they are more receptive to learning and taking academic risk. Receptive students allow teachers to deliver the knowledge that students need to go from one academic level to the next. Teachers who don't have the right temperament, desire, passion, and commitment will not be effective in an urban school, regardless of their education level, certifications, or years of teaching experience.

There are two ways to tell if you have the right teacher. First, principals must ask the right questions during the interviewing process. They must ask questions that solicit elaborate responses from perspective candidates about their deepest convictions about education, students, and the teaching-and-learning process. During the interview process, principals should seek to hire teachers that can give explanations that are genuine and moving.

If during an interview, the candidate says something that's truly moving, then she or he is probably genuine and has the compassion that it takes to work with students who present multiple challenges. When interviewing, principals should trust their intuitions and go with their gut feelings about who best fits the school and teaching position.

Second, not all principals have the luxury of hiring their entire teaching staff. Principals that are new to their school buildings usually come in with the majority of the teaching positions already filled. Also, some people are extremely good at saying the right things during an interview but may lack what it takes to be successful in the classroom.

So in cases when the staff is already in place or if a person happens to be a good interviewee, principals should set up frequent opportunities to converse with teachers about how they view their roles and responsibilities as they relate to student achievement and the school's overall success.

During these opportunities, principals should find out the persons' deepest convictions and later monitor his or her actions to see if they match up. When discrepancies arise, the principal should first try to converse with the teacher, point out the issues, and provide assistance to resolve the problems. If adequate time has been allotted to support the teacher and no significant change occurs, then the principal should actively work to remove that person from the building. The space created will open up an opportunity for someone who is willing to come in and do what is needed.

Provide Teachers With Sufficient Support

As stated, most principals do not get the opportunity to interview and hire their entire teaching staff from year to year. In many instances, urban school principals inherit their staff from the previous administration, or staff members are appointed from central office. Each person will have various skills, abilities, and knowledge. Likewise, each will need varying degrees of assistance. This is why the second component for improving academic instruction is so important, which is to provide teachers with sufficient support.

Supporting teachers can come in many forms, and it depends on the teacher who's in need of assistance. Some of the most effective ways principals can support teachers is by providing adequate resources (books, materials, articles, workshops, etc.), offering individual and group conferencing, conducting classroom visits and feedback, modeling instructional practices, and facilitating quality professional development opportunities.

Many urban school principals do not support teachers in these ways, because they're not visible within the school; they are out of touch with their teachers' general needs. They do not manage their time efficiently, so they spend the majority of their day reacting to situations, people, and events that may not have a direct relationship with improving academic instruction.

Also, there are some urban school principals who are weak instructional leaders. They intentionally avoid going into classrooms and dealing with items pertaining to instruction because they're either uncomfortable or unaware of how to observe quality instruction across an array of disciplines and provide teachers with the meaningful feedback and advice.

It should be a common practice for urban school principals to visit classrooms regularly to observe. The observations should translate into providing teachers with relevant feedback and keeping them informed about the dynamics associated with students, teachers, and the learning progression.

If the leader of the school is not sound instructionally, then there is a great possibility that the majority of the school's teachers will not be sound instructionally either. I'm not saying that principals should know the intricacies of every discipline in every grade level, but I am saying they should be able to recognize quality instruction in action and provide teachers with relevant support across various subject areas.

For example, there are principals who hold teachers to standards to which they don't hold themselves. They want teachers to create dynamic lessons that are engaging to students, but when they host professional development sessions for teachers, they lecture or pass out papers that have little value. After the first 10 to 15 minutes of hearing a principal's lecture, the majority of the audience stops paying attention.

If the professional development sessions were not required, many of the teachers would not come, because the information delivered is not presented in a way that connects with them. I know of situations where teachers have used their mandatory professional development meetings with their principals as an opportunity to grade students' papers or tests.

Urban school principals have to start viewing themselves as teachers of teachers. They have to develop their instructional leadership skills to assist teachers with improving students' academic achievement. They should view their time with teachers as a way to model what is expected within the classroom.

In addition to the other support mechanisms offered to teachers, principals should be able to demonstrate sound academic knowledge and model good teaching practices. This will help teachers improve their practice, which will result in advances in student achievement. Once principals are able to hire the right teachers and provide them with the right support, student achievement will blossom—taking the school to new academic heights.

TEN

Standardized Testing

Nearly all U.S. states have some form of standardized testing or mechanism for determining student achievement. These tests also come with certain mandates for school districts, which are linked to the school districts' overall performance ratings. Such ratings categorize school districts as being effective or ineffective and, in some cases, have a bearing on the amount of state funding they receive. In most states, a student's inability to achieve a certain score on state-approved standardized tests can prevent the student from graduating high school—regardless of the student's grade point average or attendance.

The stakes are very high for school districts to show adequate progress in student achievement, and because of this, intense pressure is felt from the central office staff to the building-level employees (i.e., principals and teachers). One of the loudest arguments from urban school employees from the building level is that state standardized tests do not adequately show the progress that their students have made over the course of a school year. For example, it is not uncommon for a ninth-grade English teacher in an urban school to have one or more students in class who are nonreaders (due to language barriers, handicap, or reading deficiencies not addressed in previous grades) or who are reading three to four grades below their current grade level. A teacher who finds himself or herself in this predicament might be able to work with the students and improve their reading levels up one or two grades, but those gains are not likely to have a significant affect when the students take the standardized test.

The students are likely to fail the test despite all the progress that they and their teachers have made during the course of that particular year. This scenario can play out in multiple grade levels and throughout multiple subject areas within an urban school—especially one with a history of failure.

A strong majority of teachers who work in urban school settings claim that their work with students is unfairly judged when standardized testing is the sole means for measuring student achievement and teacher effectiveness. They also complain that the joy of teaching and learning has been greatly diminished because they have been made to "teach to the test," instead of teaching to the actual needs and deficiencies of their students. They feel pressure from administrators to cover the breath of information on the test, but they never get to cover the information with any depth: therefore, students never master the material, nor do they really get to enjoy learning.

Urban school principals are placed in a peculiar position: they have to administer the mandates from the state while, at the same time, deal with the complaints and issues affecting school-level staff as a result. It's a battle that far too many principals lose year after year. They lose because their students are receiving subpar instruction and because their teachers are failing to close the divide between what they believe they should teach and what they are required to teach.

THE HARD TRUTH

No matter how an educator feels about standardized testing, it will be around for a long time to come. It will forever be a hot topic for public education and those working within it. Standardized testing is a politically charged issue that's ultracomplicated and touches on too many sensitive issues.

Not only is standardized testing linked to the issues mentioned here, but it is a multimillion-dollar business. The creation, distributions, and grading of these tests have a money trail that stretches far and wide; I could write a separate book on the money associated with standardized testing alone. So, standardized testing isn't going anywhere any time soon.

Despite the multitude of complaints and issues surrounding standardized testing, urban school principals can and should use it as a tool for measuring their students' progress. In fact, there is no way possible for a public school principal to avoid or opt out of administering the state's adopted test. Instead of getting on a soapbox and complaining like so many other teachers and administrators, urban school principals should develop a plan for tackling this issue. The following framework is one that urban school principals can follow to effectively deal with standardized testing.

Learn All the Parameters of the Test

Principals should gather as much information possible about the test. Some of the vital elements to understanding the test center on the following: important dates, grade levels being tested, the structure of the test (multiple choice, short answer, essay, or a mixture), time constraints, standards the test will cover, the manner in which the test will be scored, receiving the results, and the subject areas covered (to name a few).

The more principals know about the test, the better they'll be able to develop plans and remain focused on the really important items. They should search these things out for themselves and not rely totally on answers and directives from central office. Principals need a clear understanding of the test as it relates to the students and staff at their particular schools. The information gathered will serve as the foundation for successfully implementing strategies and administering the test to students.

Create Two Testing Cohorts

Even though standardized tests are administered to students yearly, principals should view the test in two-year intervals, putting the focus on students in the current testing year and those who will be tested the following year. Viewing the test from this perspective will assist principals with planning and preparation from one year to the next and will better prepare teachers and students who will be involved with the test.

For example, let's take any given state in America that administers standardized testing to its students; for the sake of this example, let's also pretend that the state issues the test to students in Grades 3, 8, and 10. Students in these grades would represent Cohort A, since those are the primary testing grades. Therefore, Cohort B will be students in Grades 2, 7, and 9, respectively, because these students are one grade level away from the primary testing grade.

After students have been divided into two cohorts, the principal must learn everything there is to know about the students in each. The information should include but not be limited to the following: attendance rates, types of disciplinary issues, strong and weak academic performers, academic strengths and weaknesses, the teachers who teach these students (including their strengths and weaknesses), and so on. This and other pertinent information is vital for the principal's planning process.

For example, if students in Cohort A are deficient in math and the top math teacher is going to be out for 12 weeks due to pregnancy, then the principal has to make an adjustment to maintain the same level of instruction while the top math teacher is way. There are a host of issues that could come up that will pertain to both cohorts of students and the teachers who teach them. The information gathered on each group will inform the principal's decision making and help to ensure that the best decisions are made for each group.

Align the Standards

The standards that teachers cover in their respective classrooms should be in alignment with standards that students will see on standardized tests. This includes but is not limited to all lesson plans, learning objectives, and classroom activities used to help students learn.

This is not teaching to the test; it's teaching to the criteria set by the state in which the school district operates. Each state in America has a board or governing body that sets standards for each subject area. The standards established are what each state wants children living within the state to learn.

School districts develop subjects and curriculum around these standards, which eventually trickles down to every school and every classroom operating within each state. If teachers are teaching something other than what the state deems appropriate for a particular subject area, then that teacher is not teaching to the state's expectations. Principals must maintain the integrity of their schools' academic programs by ensuring that the standards for each subject area are the focal point of instruction and not random, arbitrary items that have little to no connection with the test or what the state wants for its citizens.

Principals who have done their research know exactly what standards are covered for each aspect of the test. Therefore, they should be able to work with their teachers to not only create appropriate curriculums for each subject area but also align them as such to the state's standards. For example, if students will be asked to read an informational text and write a brief constructed response, then students should be given similar classroom exercises and activities in class. Similarly, if the math portion of the test is predominantly made up of algebra and geometry questions, then students should be exposed to these kinds of questions while in math class.

Also, it would be a good idea for principals to make sure that every student in the primary testing cohort is in the proper math class early in the school year. This will allow the school's administrative team to collect data on these students more accurately, determine their academic deficiencies, and provide them with the proper support and intervention before the test is administered.

Students in Cohort B will set the foundation for the next year, when they will be in the primary testing cohort. The instruction they receive should be the basis for what will be taught the following year. This will ensure that teachers are building on what students learn from one year to the next.

Some principals like to give teachers pacing guides to help them gage which standards should be covered at various points within the school year. This is a good strategy, but in doing so, the pacing guides should also allow time for teachers to reteach information not mastered by students or cover prerequisite information not mastered by students during their previous grade.

Teachers should never be forced to teach using prescribed robotic methods or be told how to teach. Doing so will stifle the teachers' creativity, which will adversely affect the quality of instruction rendered to students. Standards-based education is more about outlining what to teach instead of how to teach.

It is the principal's job to provide the framework (i.e., outlining the standards that need to be covered, providing support, and giving feedback), but teachers must retain a high level of autonomy when it comes to delivering instruction. The methods and strategies they use should be based on their professional assessment of the students' academic needs and deficiencies. Teachers should have the flexibility to teach students at their current levels and be able to build on students' prior knowledge based on the standards of any given subject area.

Schedule a Pretest Date

In most states, testing is done between the months of March and May. Therefore, the pretest date should be scheduled during the months of September through December—several months before the actual testing date. This will give principals enough time to conduct their preliminary assessment of where the students are academically and determine what interventions should be employed.

A pretesting date should be designated only for students in Cohort A because they're the ones who will be tested during a given school year, but if the principal and his or her team have their structure and organizational plans in order, then Cohort B could be given a pretest as well. The pretest should be conducted in the same manner as the real test date. This would include but not be limited to any changes in the school's schedule, possible movement of students, designation of testing areas, distribution and collection of test and materials, changes with staff schedules and duties, and so on.

This is done for several reasons: first, it gives students and staff an opportunity to practice the events that will take place on the actual testing date. Some students don't do as well as they could on standardized tests simply because they get caught up in the excitement and changes connected with the actual day of the test and the variations in their regular school day.

Some students become too antsy or anxious, or they lose focus. Giving students the opportunity to practice and go through the motions of "test day" will help them become more comfortable and relaxed when it comes time to take the test for real.

Second, a pretest helps school officials prepare for creating the right testing environment. There are many things to consider when administering a standardized test. The school's administrative team must try to plan every possible detail in advance. Something as simple as not having a plan for dealing with tardy students on test day could have serious implications on the continuity of the testing environment.

Pretests also help bring to light issues that might have been overlooked by school officials. Students, especially younger students, often view changes associated with testing as a time during their school day when they can act out and misbehave. Going through the motions will give school officials the opportunity to correct such behaviors beforehand, so they will not have to waste time doing so on the actual test day.

Last, the most important reason for scheduling a pretest date is that it gives principals opportunities to gather and analyze data. The results of the pretest can be used to provide more detailed information on the students' present levels of academic performance. The information yielded from pretests can serve as a window into the areas that should be targeted for improvement, as well as highlighting areas of strength.

Pretest data should be shared with teachers and collectively discussed to create a correct course of action for targeting students' academic deficiencies and enhancing the areas of proficiency. Pretest data could also help principals make projections as to how students will fair when they actually have to take the test.

Hire a Testing Coordinator

A testing coordinator is an essential component that urban schools must have to move out of academic failure. The person hired or appointed for this position must handle all things related to testing; it is her or his primary focus and the means by which one will be evaluated. This position is very important because the principal will not have time, due to a host of other responsibilities, to carry out the day-to-day tasks associated test coordination.

The testing coordinator's focus should include but not be limited to the following: gathering information and related data, addressing students' and teachers' needs (in both cohorts), knowing significant dates, being familiar with academic interventions and available resources, administering and collecting tests (pretest and actual test), addressing personnel associated with the testing process, gathering and distributing testing-related information, and sharing information with various stakeholders, to name just a few.

This person should work closely with the principal regarding the planning process and should be part of all test-related school-based committees and meetings. The person occupying this position should not have many responsibilities outside those that are testing related. If the principal doesn't have the luxury of hiring a testing coordinator, then he or she should appoint an assistant principal or staff leader.

If an assistant principal is appointed, he or she should not be bogged down with too many issues that would take him or her away from performing the important duties related to testing (hall duty, student discipline, book distribution, bus detail, etc.). The menial tasks normally performed by this person should be given to another assistant principal or delegated to other people on the staff.

If using an assistant principal is not an option, then one of the staff leaders should be appointed. A staff leader is someone who stands out from the others due to one's work ethic and job acumen. This person could be a teacher, counselor, psychologist, reading specialist, instructional coach, and so on.

Staff leaders usually have experience and are reliable, effective at their craft, and respected by others on the staff. Some of the best candidates for a test coordinator position are those who aspire to enter the school administrative ranks or those who don't mind taking on more responsibility. If the testing coordinator comes from ranks of the certified staff leaders and not from the assistant principal pool, then his or her schedule should be modified so that he or she can have time to perform the tasks associated with testing. For example, if a teacher is appointed as the coordinator, he or she could be given a teaching schedule that's half a regular teacher's assignment or, at the very least, be given an extra planning period and be relieved of the menial tasks assigned to teachers that are outside classroom instruction (hall duty, lunch detail, after-school clubs, etc.). The testing coordinator is a vital position. Principals should select this person very carefully and be clear about the expectations needing to be carried out.

Establish a Before- or After-School Tutoring Program

As mentioned previously, some of the students who are part of the primary testing cohort could be several academic levels below where they should be. The reasons for this vary, but principals shouldn't be as concerned about why students are behind; rather, they should be more concerned about what they're going to do to raise students' achievement to functional levels.

Not all interventions should be targeted during classroom instructional time. Having teachers spend too much time on material that should have been covered three or four grades ago may not necessarily be a good use of their time. Besides, there could be students that are on par or functioning above grade level for whom the teacher has to provide a quality education as well.

Some of the work that students do and the work that teachers need to do must take place before or after school. Teachers can use the before- or after-school time to deal specifically with students' deficiencies or teach content that students should have learned in previous grades. Principals must be very selective in choosing the teachers for the tutoring sessions.

The teachers selected should be the ones who are not only good at teaching their particular content areas but can excite students and keep their interest. The teachers who are the most engaging will be the ones to whom the students will respond. If students do not have any connection with the teachers conducting the tutoring sessions, then they will not attend or behave long enough for the sessions to be of any value to them.

Final note about using tutoring as an intervention: schools should offer this intervention to all students that need it, but the reality is that many students will not voluntarily show up for the tutoring sessions for various reasons. Therefore, principals will have to be very creative in thinking of ways that will encourage students to attend, as well as inform parents of the necessity. The parents have to be involved in this process.

If parents are in agreement with the intervention being provided and understand the necessity of it, then there is a high probability that students will attend whether the session is held before or after school. Principals must think outside the box regarding how to entice students to take advantage of the extra help. The information outlined in previous chapters will assist with devising ways to do that. The methods that principals use must be relative to each school and to the interests of the students and parents involved.

Even though the tutoring sessions are open to all students in the targeted grade levels (Cohorts A and B), there should be concentrated efforts made by principals and tests coordinators to target students who are in the "middle of the pack" in terms of their academic performance. Most principals make the mistake of putting most of their attention on the students who are either advanced or low functioning (with most of the attention being placed on the latter). Students that are on target or on the brink of being on target typically do not get much attention.

Principals should direct the majority of their time, resources, efforts, people, and energy toward the "middle of the pack" students. Putting the most focus on this segment of the student population will give principals the most "bang for their buck" because there are typically more students who fall into this category than any other.

These students are the ones who attend school regularly, so they will benefit the most from the academic instruction and interventions. These students will also show the most academic gains over the shortest amount of time, which will drastically improve the failure rate on the standardized test. The middle-pack students are also the ones who typically have the least behavior, social, emotional, and academic problems.

I've found that doctors take a similar approach when treating burn victims. Individuals who are burned over 80 percent of their bodies receive only enough support and attention from doctors to sustain their lives. More resources are administered if an individual in this condition shows increased signs of life.

No one knows why some victims who are severely burned are able to recover while others are not, but it starts with the patient's intrinsic desire and resilience to stay alive. As burn victims show increased signs of improvement, doctors will gradually increase their support and medical resources until the victim makes a full recovery.

This is done because doctors know from research and experience that individuals who are burned severely have a very low chance of survival. Since resources are limited, it would not be cost-effective to use the bulk of the resources on those who might not survive to begin with.

Burn victims who enter the emergency room with less than 50 percent of their bodies burned will receive the bulk of the resources and the doctor's attention. Individuals who are not severely burned have the best chances of survival, so they get the full extent of any treatments the hospital has available. Doctors have learned over time that individuals who are burned on less than half their bodies not only have the highest probability for survival but also heal the fastest.

Urban school principals should follow the same course of action when administering the standardized test to students. The students who are in the middle of the pack academically do not typically have as many deficiencies. These students will be able to make advances quickly, so the bulk of the resources should be geared toward them.

This doesn't mean principals should neglect or ignore students who are at the bottom of the curve. All students have a right to any and all services provided by the school, but due to the multitude of deficiencies that the low-end students have, any academic gains they might achieve will not register on the test.

Furthermore, many of the students in this category have home lives and environmental situations that have contributed to their academic problems. These students and their parents will typically be the ones who will put up the most resistance and neglect to take advantage of the resources offered.

Some students' academic deficiencies, parental support and home environment, and socioemotional status are too far out of the realm of what's needed to be successful. The assistance needed to save them from this condition is beyond the reach of public education; the system was not designed to handle such deficiencies, nor does it have the proper funding, resources, and personnel to do so.

This is why it is more prudent for urban school principals to concentrate on meeting the needs of students who stand in the middle of the academic curve. These are the students who will help bring the school out of academic failure the fastest.

The Principal's Actions

Everything that happens within the school setting begins and ends with the principal. The principal is not able to shift the responsibility to anyone else. Therefore, he or she must approach standardized testing with enormous focus and intensity. The principal's attitude and the mental energy devoted to this area will have a significant bearing on the final test results and will set the tone for how the rest of the staff will approach testing as well.

The planning, preparations, and structures implemented by the principal to support the testing process will help other staff members perform their jobs more effectively, which will increase the students' chances for success. The principal must always plan ahead, constantly looking for gaps, weaknesses, and ways to improve the process, whether in scheduling, personnel, structurally, or budget allocations.

To do this, principals must implement two key tactics: conduct classroom observations and analyze summative assessment data. This will give them an accurate pulse of what is and is not happening within the classroom setting. The two tactics will also point out adjustments to make and ways to maximize resources.

If principals want to move student achievement forward, they have be a constant presence in the classrooms, where teaching and learning take place. They need to view with their own eyes the dynamics of the classroom and the interactions between teachers and students.

Principals need firsthand knowledge about how instruction is delivered to students; therefore, they should make it a habit of visiting multiple classrooms during various times of day. This will help them develop a global view of the quality of instruction that takes place throughout the school. The observations should also yield regular and timely feedback to teachers, which will help them to improve their teaching practices.

After the observations and feedback, principals should regularly collect summative assessment data from teachers in every core academic subject area to judge how well students understand the lessons being taught. This type of data is typically generated from tests given to students at the end of a unit before going to the next set of standards. If the summative assessment data doesn't show a positive pass rate on any given set of assessments collected, then it would be a clear indicator that students didn't master that set of standards and materials.

Summative assessment data will prompt principals to look into the factors that are causing low performance. They should try to come up with answers to the following questions: Is there something wrong with the teachers' instructional delivery? Is student attendance affecting the assessment results? Is the teacher's classroom management affecting the level to instruction? Are there too many student discipline issues occurring in classrooms? Are we testing enough students? Are more resources needed? Should the teacher go back and reteach the unit?

There could be a host of reasons why achievement is low on a given summative assessment or set of assessments. It is up to the principal and his or her administrative team to find out why the results are low and to do something about it.

Analyzing summative assessment data will help principals discover tends, strengths, and weaknesses. It will also help them make adjustments to the process as related to the academic needs of students. If some teachers are having good results and others are not, principals can capture what the stronger teachers are doing and share those methods with the teachers who are in need of support. This will help strengthen the overall instructional program throughout the entire school.

When it comes to standardized testing, principals must operate in a continual cycle of conducting observation, offering feedback, analyzing data, targeting students' needs, and making adjustments. This cycle should be perpetuated until the day of the actual test. Principals must use the information obtained from the observations and assessment data to push forward, hold people accountable, and create a sense of urgency.

As the school's leader, the principal has the power to set the pace for everyone within the school. Principals must constantly take action that moves instruction forward and everyone else associated with it.

Final note about standardized testing: there are many principals who are getting into trouble over the validity of their schools' test scores. There have been several large school districts located in major U.S. urban cities that have been in the national news and accused of cheating. The schools in question were caught because the students' scan sheets contained too many eraser marks.

The investigating entities reported that the schools' officials were changing students' wrong answers into correct ones. Some of the stories I've read regarding this unethical practice involved elaborate schemes, which included principals and multiple building-level and central office employees working together to make it look as if students were doing academically better than what they really were.

In most urban school districts, especially ones with a history of failure, the pressure to improve test scores is very intense. Jobs and reputations are at stake, and some districts are even offering monetary incentives for principals and teachers whose students perform well. This intensifies the pressure and creates the climate that causes some people to do anything in their power to show higher results, whether the students are advancing or not.

Educators who cheat on standardized tests have it all wrong: cheating is not the way to improve test scores. The reality is that when you cheat, the people who are cheated the most are the students because they aren't being provided with a quality education.

What's the significance of having a high score on a test if students are not able to read and write? To improve test scores and move student achievement forward, you must improve the quality of instruction. If instruction improves, student achievement and test scores will follow.

ELEVEN
Central Office Staff

It is no secret that many principals in urban schools have issues and complaints about central office staff. The complaints are indicative of each principal's temperament and each school district's culture. The following is a short list of some of the more common complaints that principals have of central office employees:

- Too many people from central office are trying to tell principals how to run their schools—most of whom have never served as principal and are not in a supervisory capacity over building principals.
- Central office personnel are too far removed from what actually goes on in urban schools and what the actual responsibilities of principals are.
- Central office personnel push too much unnecessary paperwork and mandates on principals.
- The people in central office never take the time to find out what principals in urban schools really need, want, or desire before making decisions that will affect the way that principals operate their schools.
- Principals need more control and authority, which some people in central office refuse to relinquish. Principals need more freedom and autonomy to operate their schools effectively.
- There is an overall lack of support from central office.

This list is not an exhaustive one. It merely serves some examples that highlight the disconnection between principals and central office personnel. This is a huge problem within many urban school districts that's commonly overlooked. The disconnection often contributes to the overall dysfunction and inefficiency of the entire school district.

Chapter 11

THE HARD TRUTH

Despite all the complaints by principals about central office personnel, principals still need to be cordial and work toward building solid relationships with them as they would any other stakeholder. There are several reasons why the two groups should work cooperatively with each other. Some of the more obvious are as follows: both groups are employed by the same school district and should work together on the common goal of educating students, supporting parents, and serving the surrounding communities.

It is more advantageous for principals to initiate good relations with central office employees because in some urban school districts, especially those with over 30,000 students, many central office personnel will never get to know anything about certain schools or the principals who operate them, aside from what they read on some spreadsheet or from what others in central office have to say. If principals act rude, disrespectful, or uncooperative to central office personnel, those messages will be spread to others in central office, which could have an adverse impact on the principals' school or their ability to get things done.

There are people in central office that have miniscule positions in relation to building-level principals, but those same people serve individuals that are in higher positions. Oftentimes, they have the ears of those who can make life easy or difficult for principals.

There are principals who always get the best resources and support and receive timely information. These principals have no problems with making positive things happen for their schools. Part of the reason is that they've taken the time to establish rapport with those who can push things through for them and look out for their best interests.

Yet, there are principals who never receive (or they're last in line to get) needed support and resources for their schools. For example, they can never figure out why their documents never make it off someone's desk for processing or why items they request never arrive in a timely manner. They wonder why they always experience delays and derailments.

Part of the reason why the unsuccessful principals are in such bad shape is that they haven't made an effort to build solid relationships with central office staff. In some extreme cases, the bonds that principals form with central office staff not only make the difference with getting things processed more quickly but could mean the difference between the principal remaining employed or not.

TWELVE

The School's Budget

Most people in society are unaware of the enormous amounts of money that it takes to run a successful school district. Even those working in education often take the resources available to them for granted (technology, furniture, equipment, salaries, supplies, human capital, etc.). The reality is that every pencil, chair, light bulb, trash can, computer, chalkboard, desk, paper clip, copier, paper towel, bath tissue, and every other resource were once a line item on the school's budget.

All programs and personnel rely on the stability of the school's budget. It is imperative that urban school principals gain a keen understanding of how the school district spends money, as well as gain as much control as possible of the various aspects of the budgetary process.

Urban school principals should have an astute understanding of all programs and personnel needs within the school, including how much or how little is needed for each to work effectively. Principals should have the knowledge and wherewithal to apply the school's financial resources in the most applicable manner.

THE HARD TRUTH

Most school districts today do not give principals the autonomy to make their schools' budgeting decisions. In some districts, school budget allocations are done from the central office level, or committees are set up to share in the decision-making process with principals. In some extreme cases, the committee acts as a governing body, and the principal must get the committee's approval before moving forward.

Such measures have been put in place for several reasons: some principals have abused their authority over the school's budget, made poor financial decisions, or behaved unethically. Others have made decisions based on their friendships, networks, and acquaintances with various stakeholders, instead of making decisions based on the needs of the school. But in trying to minimize the damage from incompetent or neglectful principals, school districts have created another problem—split decision making.

Split decision making happens when you have individuals with relatively the same level of power and authority trying to make decisions over limited resources. In many instances, the individuals who are part of these committees overstep their boundaries and start inserting themselves in areas where they shouldn't. In some extreme cases, they have ventured into curriculum and personnel decisions.

Split decision making is the fastest way to render a principal ineffective and leave a school submerged in mediocrity or failure, especially when it comes to using money designated for school operations. It is hard for all parties with equal authority to form a consensus on the important issues, because all are lobbying use to the budget for their own interests and not the greater interest of the entire school.

Principals are the ones being held accountable for the school's success or failure, so they should rightfully have the most control. I'm not advocating that urban school principals shouldn't listen to the advice or suggestions of other stakeholders, nor should they deny others with vested interests the opportunities to share in some part of the decision-making process. But I am saying that principals should be given the final say on how school funds should be spent. For principals to be effective in their positions, they must seek to gain as much control over their schools' budgets as possible.

If a principal is in a district where most of the budget decisions are made from central office, then the principal must actively work to become familiar with those making most of the decisions about his or her school to become part of the decision-making process. Reaching out early and often to the persons that handle budgetary items will increase the principal's chances of being able to give input and make suggestions on how the school's money should be spent.

If a principal is working in a district where he or she has to get approval from a site-based committee, then he or she has to be more diligent. In some urban schools, it's hard for a principal to allocate funds appropriately because the committees are so disjointed. Most of the site-based committees in urban schools do not operate as a cohesive unit, so it makes it extremely hard for them to arrive at a consensus on most issues, especially those involving the school's budget.

The only way to effectively operate with a fractional and disjointed committee is for principals to work to bring the committee together under a shared vision. This is done by exhibiting leadership and establishing trust among the committee members. In situations like this, principals must articulate a clear vision to all stakeholders and lead all discussions involving the school's interconnected parts; therefore, he or she can direct the committee's discussions on the school's budgeting needs as they relate to staff, students, program, supplies, and building maintenance. Solid leadership and trust building is the antidote for keeping site-based decision committees from running amuck.

When the principal is involved with any school-based committee, the members of such will have a natural tendency to look toward the principal for leadership. The principal is usually seen as the expert on all school-related issues. Committees that break into fractions and lobby for their own self-interests do so when principals fail to step up and lead.

When principals are nonresponsive, aloof, weak, passive, quiescent, and void of information, the committee members will lose confidence and think they have to insert themselves to fill the leadership void. Remember: most site-based committee members are made of people who have a great deal invested in the school for various reasons. If they think that the principal lacks what it takes to get things done, they will begin to split into fractions, which will create power struggles within the group.

This will create a climate of disconnectedness, turmoil, bickering, mistrust, and confusion. Since many of the committee members don't have intimate knowledge about the school's overall needs, a good portion of their decisions will not be aligned. This creates more dysfunction and contributes to a school's overall inefficiency and failure.

Principals that are out in front and responsive to stakeholders tend to inspire confidence and respect. Then when it's time to make budgeting decisions, the committee members are more willing to go along with the principal's ideas and suggestions. This also maintains the committee's cohesiveness and ensures that the school's resources are spent in a manner that best serves the needs of the school.

THIRTEEN
Social Media

We now live in a world where information is being transmitted and broadcasted within seconds of an actual event. There used to be a time when people received news and information from a few primary sources: radio, television, and newspapers. Now people receive the most current information via the Internet, smartphones, and social media.

Some of the most popular social outlets used today are Facebook, Twitter, YouTube, and MySpace. These social websites and others like them are used to build networks where people can communicate and stay connected. Even the business and entertainment sectors have gravitated to this phenomenon, using it to stay in touch with their customer and fan bases.

Urban schools shouldn't be the exception when it comes to using social media. They should also use it to connect with their customer bases. The customer bases for urban schools are the parents and the members of the community where students live. Utilizing social networks will help to close the distance that often exists between urban schools and the communities they serve. It will also help schools to dispense accurate information to community members regarding school events, programs, and occurrences.

THE HARD TRUTH

Somehow, urban schools are the last to get on board with using technology and tapping into the benefits of social media. This goes back to the deep-rooted conservatism imbedded in public education and the fear that's associated with systemic change.

The truth is that principals who are able to connect with stakeholders in multiple ways will be the most effective. Using social media is a great means for the school to communicate with the community and for the community to communicate with the school. The reciprocal communication will provide schools with better means for staying abreast of what's going on in the community and for informing the community about what's going on in the school—making both parties well informed and connected.

The messages communicated through social media can also be used to combat some of the negative press that urban schools receive from traditional media outlets and to help change negative perceptions that the public may have about the school.

Many times, urban schools are behind the curve when it comes to implementing technology and adapting innovations that greater society has embraced. Urban school principals need to be proactive and constantly seek ways to use new technology and social media for the betterment of their schools.

FOURTEEN

Practice Self-Reflection

There is a multitude of high-level decisions that urban school principals have to make, equaled by the number of emergency situations that seem to appear out of nowhere. A principal of an urban high school once shared with me that in one week, she had four student fights, one fire (a group of students set fire to the contents of a trash can in the girl's restroom), one death (a 58-year-old security guard collapsed in the hallway due to a massive heart attack), and the discovery of a loaded gun located in a student's locker, which brought local police and television and newspaper reporters to the school. All of this took place while a potential walkout of teachers loomed due to contract negotiation breakdowns between the teachers' union and the school district's superintendent.

Things can happen so rapidly that urban school principals will often find themselves engaged in one major issue after another—constantly testing their mettle and leadership abilities. This is why it is very important for urban school principals to practice self-reflection. *Webster's* defines *reflection* as one's ability to contemplate on an idea or think seriously about something. In reference to the urban school principalship, self-reflection is the process of taking time to think about previous experiences and situations that happen within the school setting.

Reflecting on past experiences is a way for principals to assess themselves and the decisions they make while on the job. It allows them to think back on initiatives, confrontations, interactions, methods, and all other occurrences associated with the principalship and the responsibilities thereof.

It also allows one to ask the serious questions: Did I handle the situation in the best manner possible? Were my actions and words befitting the circumstances? Could I have done something differently? Should I have been more understanding and compassionate? How can I improve in this area? What could I have done to make the situation better? Did my actions help or hurt the situation? Do I have enough desire to remain effective in this position? Did I act in a fair and unbiased manner?

No matter how intelligent, talented, skillful, charismatic, democratic, or visionary one might be as a school leader, it is very easy to make a mistake in the high-stakes environment of urban education. Urban school principals are inundated with high-priority decisions on a daily basis. It is not humanly possible to respond perfectly to all people and situations encountered. So if a mistake is made in some manner, principals should reflect on the matter and try to learn from it.

The purpose of self-reflection is not for urban school principals to start second-guessing themselves or become ultraconservative. The overarching goal of self-reflection is for principals to give an honest assessment of themselves. Whenever they are confronted with a similar situation, they will know how to respond appropriately or at least have a framework for making the best-informed decision.

REFLECT ON PAST EVENTS

For self-reflection to be of any real value, urban school principals must do two things: reflect on past events while away from the school and be completely honest. First, it is good practice for principals to self-reflect while being away from the school. While physically at the school, principals are engulfed by the environment and surrounded by various situations, people, and events. They have to step out of the environment to clear the mental space needed to properly assess themselves.

It is also good to let some time elapse before reflecting on an intense situation (irate parents, disruptive students, critical conversations, disciplinary issues with the staff, etc.). While the intense situation or event is fresh in the principal's mind, his or her emotions will be viscerally tied to that event. Being at an emotionally high level will not allow principals to properly assess their actions and behavior. They need to let their emotions cool down before they can contemplate on the event in a way that's most beneficial for them.

Personally, I take time to reflect at the end of each workweek. I recount in my mind nearly every significant detail of my actions—everything from conversations to the types of assistance provided to individuals. I scrutinize myself with the same intense level that I use to evaluate other aspects of the school. What I found is that by reflecting on past events, I became more focused and sharp. Just as I've set the bar high for others within the school, I equally hold myself accountable to the same standard or greater.

BE HONEST WITH YOURSELF

Urban school principals must be honest when assessing themselves. It's easy to look at the work of others in the school's community and critique, evaluate, cavil, or place judgment, but it takes a courageous individual to look honestly at oneself with a critical eye. Some urban school principals might have a problem with honestly assessing themselves because they might not like what they see.

Their honest reflection might reveal that they could be doing a lot more. They could give more effort, take on more tough issues, listen more to key stakeholders, and be more responsive. They might have to make some personal changes that might not fit within their comfort levels. Some principals fool themselves into believing that they're doing a good job, but the condition of the school and its staff says otherwise. If a person is unable to be honest with himself or herself, then self-reflection will not be useful.

It is also a good practice for urban school principals to confide in a colleague or mentor—preferably, one not working in the same school district—who understands the intricacies of the position and to use that person's feedback as a form of self-assessment. The mentor/colleague might be able to offer an alternative view or introduce a perspective that would have otherwise been missed. Urban school principals must be able to assess themselves and their practices for what they truly are. This is the only way that any real personal growth can be attained.

One final note: when engaged in deep reflection, one will often recall many of the positive experiences. Positive reflections are good for principals because they serve as the fuel needed for rejuvenation when things are not going as smoothly as they should. In the often lonely, unpredictable, and stress-filled world of the urban school principal, the good memories are there to not only learn from but to serve as the motivation for moving onward.

Conclusion

Throughout the pages of this book, I speak in great detail about real problems, people, and issues that stand in the way of true reform for urban schools. I wrote this book for urban school principals because I think that the leadership has the greatest potential for making the necessary changes for transforming urban schools into successful institutions for students and staff.

Despite the practical and candid nature of this book, I would be remiss if I failed to mention the role that poverty plays in all of this. Poverty—and the affect that it has on the people suffering from it—is the greatest factor plaguing urban education.

Numerous studies have shown poverty to be linked with poor performance in academics, low IQ scores, and increased risk of students dropping out of school. The issues of poor student achievement, low teacher morale and retention, disruptive students, stagnation, inefficiency, unsupportive parents, and disorganization are all symptoms caused by long-term poverty.

Schools are nothing more than an extension of the communities they serve; therefore, the communities' problems will undoubtedly become the schools' problems in most situations. This phenomenon is not isolated to urban schools. The same holds true for all institutions that serve low socioeconomically deprived communities. It doesn't matter if it's health care, housing, transportation, or business; any institution that serves the poor and disadvantaged is likely to mirror some of the same problems affecting the people in the communities where they live.

As communities where urban students live deteriorate, so too do the schools they attend. One of the greatest questions facing America today is this: what can be done to fight poverty? The answer has great implications for public education, urban schools, and the entire country as a whole. If politicians and government officials fail to handle the issue of poverty swiftly and accurately, public education as we know it could be a thing of the past.

I say this because America was founded on the premise that any person, regardless of his or her financial standing in life, could climb up the socioeconomic ladder with a little sweat and hard work. There was a time in America when industries were thriving, unemployment was low, and there was relative prosperity and success. Although it was not perfect, the country's public educational system was also ranked among the best in the world. All of these factors combined gave people hope in the American dream.

Today, many of the factories and industries that once fueled America's economy are nonexistent, or they've moved aboard—enticed by cheaper labor and increased profits. The jobs that were once plentiful for America's citizens are now minuscule. Millions of Americans are living check to check, or they're struggling to meet their basic needs. The public educational system has fallen from being ranked number one. It is now ranked 26th among other industrialized nations. The American dream has somehow turned into a nightmare.

It's no coincidence that the blunt of the criticism and blame for the decline of America's public educational system points directly at urban schools. These schools predominantly serve the highest concentrations of black and minority students. The students who come from these families live at or below the poverty line.

The communities where they live are plagued with drugs, violence, and unemployment. Many of the students living in these communities are deprived of one or more of their basic physical needs: food, clothing, shelter, or safety. Some might be missing one or more of their psychological or emotional needs as well.

Many critics of urban education often blame teachers, administrators, parents, or students for the current state of urban schools. They often try to remedy the problems by using tactics such as teacher pay-for-performance contracts, districtwide uniform policies for students, or increased student behavioral policies. These commonly used tactics are just as useless as they are disconnected from the real issues and reasons why minorities in urban schools are performing at lower levels academically.

It is my belief that schools that serve families of low economic status are not inherently bad. The issues that make urban schools bad or not conducive for students and school staff are directly related to poverty on every level. Decreasing poverty will automatically improve urban schools and improve the overall quality for people in the communities the schools serve.

Public education and urban schools in general were never set up to handle such gross dysfunction. It was never intended to deal with so many deficiencies on so many levels. Many of the strategies mentioned for principals are shaped by the environment they have to contend with. Principals working in nonurban districts don't have to even think about some of the problems mentioned in this book because their setting is entirely different.

I truly believe that urban schools can do many things better. I also believe that principals can and will play a vital role in the transformation. But for America's public educational system to really move to the next level and regain the prominence it once had, there has to be a conscious effort to decrease poverty and increase the quality of education for poor and minorities.

This expanding segment of America's population offer untapped pools of human capital and resources that could be used for the country's benefit. America can no longer afford to function with only a select few of its citizens receiving a quality education; it can no longer afford to have only a few citizens become wealthy while the majority struggle to get by and make ends meet.

America must return to the principles it was founded on and provide equal opportunities for all of its citizens. The opportunities must be educational as well as financial—intellectual as well as economic. If these opportunities are not forthcoming, America's worst problems could be yet to come. Now that's the Hard Truth.

Bibliography

Barth, R. (1990). *Improving Schools from Within*. San Francisco: Jossey-Bass.
Bonnie, D. (2006). *How to Teach Students Who Don't Look like You*. Thousand Oaks, CA: Corwin Press.
Buffum, A., & Hinman, C. (2006). Professional learning communities: Reigniting passion and purpose. *Leadership, 35*(5), 16–19.
Colvin, G. (2007). *Seven Steps toward Developing a Proactive Schoolwide Discipline Plan*. Thousand Oaks, CA: Corwin Press.
Daresh, J. (2006). *Beginning the Principalship: A Practical Guide for New School Leaders*. Thousand Oaks, CA: Corwin Press.
Downs, A. (2000). *The Fearless Executive: Find the Courage to Trust Your Talents and Be the Leader You Are Meant to Be*. New York: AMACOM.
Erb, T. O., & Stevenson, C. (1999). From faith to facts: Turning points in action—What difference does teaming make? *Middle School Journal, 30*(3), 47–50.
Ferlazzo, L., & Hammond, L. (2009). *Building Parent Engagement in Schools*. Santa Barbara, CA: Linworth Books.
Howard, T., Dresser, S., & Dunklee, D. (2009). *Poverty Is Not a Learning Disability: Equalizing Opportunities for Low SES Students*. Thousand Oaks, CA: Corwin Press.
Jones, F. (2007). *Tools for Teaching*. Fred H. Jones.
Marzano, R. (2003). *What Works in Schools: Translating Research into Action*. Alexandria, VA: ASCD.
Patterson, K., Grenny, J., McMillan, R., & Switzler, A. (2002). *Crucial Conversations: Tools for Talking When Stakes Are High*. New York: McGraw-Hill.
Paulo, F. (2000). *Pedagogy of the Oppressed* (30th ed.). New York: Continuum.
Payne, R. (2005). *A Framework for Understanding Poverty*. Highlands, TX: aha! Process.
———. (2006). *Working with Parents and Building Relationships for Student Success*. Highlands, TX: aha! Process.
Peterson, K., & Deal, T. (2009). *The Shaping School Culture Field Book* (2nd ed.). San Francisco: Jossey-Bass.
Reeves, D. (2002). *The Daily Disciplines of Leadership*. San Francisco: Jossey-Bass.
Robbins, P., & Alvy, H. (2003). *The Principal's Companion: Strategies and Hints to Make the Job Easier*. Thousand Oaks, CA: Corwin Press.
Sergiovanni, T. (1999). *Building Community in Schools*. San Francisco: Jossey-Bass.
Seyfarth, J. (1999). *The Principal: New Leadership for New Challenges*. Upper Saddle River, NJ: Prentice Hall.
Warrell, M. (2009). *Finding Your Courage: 12 Acts for Becoming Fearless at Work and in Life*. New York: McGraw-Hill.
Whitaker, T. (2002). *Dealing with Difficult Teachers* (2nd ed.). Larchmont, NY: Eye on Education.
Whitaker, T., & Fiore, D. (2001). *Dealing with Difficult Parents: And with Parents in Difficult Situations*. Larchmont, NY: Eye on Education.
Wiles, J., & Bondi, J. (1998). *Curriculum Development: A Guide to Practice*. Upper Saddle River, NJ: Prentice Hall.
Wood, T., & McCarthy, C. (2002). Understanding and preventing teacher burnout. *ERIC Digest*.
Yisrael, S. (2009). *The Positive Impact Interdisciplinary Teaming Has on Teacher Morale*. Saarbrücken, Germany: VDM.

Young, P. (2004). *You Have to Go to School—You're the Principal: 101 Tips to Make It Better for Your Students, Your Staff, and Yourself.* Thousand Oaks, CA: Corwin Press.

About the Author

Sean B. Yisrael began his career as a high school social studies teacher, where he worked in an urban school district for seven years. In 2004, he moved into school administration—holding positions in school districts located in Ohio and Washington, DC. In 2010, Dr. Yisrael formed Educational Practitioners for Better Schools, a professional development company designed to provide low-cost professional development services for school districts that have trouble providing quality training for teachers, administrators, and parents. Dr. Yisrael is a lecturer, scholar, and an author, but most importantly, he is an educator who is passionate about delivering a high quality education to students. Dr. Yisrael is the author of *12 Laws of Urban School Leadership: A Principal's Guide for Initiating Effective Change* (2012) and *Classroom Management: A Guide for Urban School Teachers* (2012), both published by Rowman & Littlefield Education.

www.ingramcontent.com/pod-product-compliance
Lightning Source LLC
Chambersburg PA
CBHW030148240426
43672CB00005B/315